"For most of human history, art-making ⸻ ⸻ ⸻ ⸻
of honoring and dialoguing with the ⸻
we often forget that our creative visior
possession; it is a verb that ties us into
our ecologies. In *The Place of All Possibilit*
an answer to this desaturated worldvie
animistic view of Jewish mysticism an
beckons us to return to our depths, the
creative spring that welcomes microbes anu rootlets alongside
dazzling angels and perplexing midrash."
— **Sophie Strand**, author of *The Flowering Wand: Rewilding the Sacred Masculine* and *The Madonna Secret*

"*The Place of All Possibility* underscores the transformative power of creativity as a means of self-discovery, healing, and connection to a deeper spiritual dimension. Rabbi Adina Allen's personal experiences illustrate the profound impact that creative expression can have on navigating challenges and accessing inner wisdom. She dismantles the common misconception that creativity is exclusive to artists, emphasizing instead that creativity is a fundamental human capacity accessible to everyone. Rabbi Allen emphasizes the communal nature of creativity and the wisdom that comes from creating from the heart. This book encourages readers to embrace creativity as a means of self-discovery, personal growth, and contributing to the collective construction of a more meaningful and connected world."
— **Susan Magsamen**, bestselling co-author of *Your Brain on Art: How the Arts Transform Us*

"This book is a window into the sacred methodology of the Jewish Studio Process, which invites us into a multidirectional process of discovery — of Torah and of self. In this time of so much heartache, when the world conspires to have us shut down, Rabbi Allen inspires us to 'make art about it' — to unlock the creative possibilities that call out from our ancient texts and traditions, and that reside in each of us. *The Place of All Possibility* is beautiful and heart-opening."
— **Rabbi Sharon Brous**, author of *The Amen Effect: Ancient Wisdom to Mend Our Broken Hearts and World*

"In this book, you are likely to encounter words. However, if you lean in closer and bend your ears towards the pages, you might come to touch something else lurking between and behind every font: a stirring sermon in turbulent times; a song, offered with such delicate dexterity, reminding us that the world is never finished, never still, and that creation is still happening now. Rabbi Allen's studious and reverent reformulation of the Torah as not just a going up on mountains, not just a taking in of instructions, but a coming down to earth, a revitalization of the ordinary with a strange potency, drips with agency. Every morsel of Rabbi Allen's disarmingly affecting invitation will spirit you away through ruptures and fissures to more wondrous delights than we can name. More than words can capture."
— **Bàyò Akómoláfé**, PhD, *These Wilds Beyond Our Fences: Letters to My Daughter on Humanity's Search for Home*

"Rabbi Adina Allen awakens our perception, revealing Imagination as an inspired process, from the Divine. Here, creativity is not constructed but received in a deep sacred dialogue. Bravo for this renewal of the possibility and purpose of arts and artful living!"
— **Lisa Miller**, PhD, Professor of Psychology and Education at Columbia University and bestselling author of *The Awakened Brain: The New Science of Spirituality and Our Quest for an Inspired Life*

"Deeply, gently, and courageously countercultural, this book is a stunning affirmation of life. In a time of narrowing imagination, Rabbi Adina Allen invites us to explore the untapped possibilities that live within us. In a time of relentless consumerism, she invites us to experience the sheer joy of creativity. In a time of shallow relevance, she invites us to listen for the layered resonance of ancient words. In a time of cynicism, she invites us to enter the *place of all possibility*. To open this book is to open oneself to hope."
— **Rabbi Sharon Cohen Anisfeld**, President of Hebrew College

"*The Place of All Possibility* is a potent call to reclaim creativity as sacred practice. Rabbi Adina Allen offers us a wise and beautiful companion for the journey — an invitation to turn towards the untamed places in our hearts, a catalyst for rewilding our spiritual lives."
— **Rabbi Julia Watts Belser**, author of *Loving Our Own Bones: Disability Wisdom and the Spiritual Subversiveness of Knowing Ourselves Whole*

"Rabbi Adina Allen's embrace of the Torah offers ways of reading and responding that align with the sacred book's embodiment of the eternal creative process — forever made anew through imaginative responses. 'Turn it and turn it, for everything is in it' affirms interpretation as a creative act, reliably a few steps ahead of the reflecting mind. What better way to demonstrate the imaginative basis of creation than engaging the hallowed text, not with authoritative fixity, but as a living and moving presence inviting 'wild' artistic and unique interpretations, embedding its voice in our lives."
— **Shaun McNiff**, author of *Trust the Process: An Artist's Guide to Letting Go* and *Imagination in Action: Secrets for Unleashing Creative Expression*

"In this lovely and insightful book, Rabbi Adina Allen uncovers the creativity that animates Jewish tradition, and gives us the tools to unleash our own creativity and reanimate our lives. Her warmth, passion, and wisdom illuminate every page."
— **Sarah Hurwitz**, author of *Here All Along: Finding Meaning, Spirituality, and a Deeper Connection to Life — in Judaism (After Finally Choosing to Look There)*

"Rabbi Adina Allen's Jewish Studio Process is the spiritual practice that will revolutionize Judaism. This practice puts the Torah of Creativity — for the first time in Jewish history — into the hands of every one of us, Jewish or not. In this book, Rabbi Allen teaches us how to unleash the power of creativity, guiding us to not only apply our insights to tradition to make it better, but to understand ourselves more fully and transform the challenges of our lives into wisdom."
— **Rabbi Benay Lappe**, President and Rosh Yeshiva of svara

"A teacher once told me, 'God is in the details,' and that is what I feel *The Place of All Possibility* aims to teach us. This is a powerful, midrashic, and visionary book."
— **Siona Benjamin**, artist and illustrator of *The Zodiac Floor* and *I Am Hava*

"In this warm, wise, and winsomely written book, Rabbi Adina Allen invites us to become creators of worlds — to engage the texts of Torah with everything we are, and to express our deepest selves by unleashing our inner creativity. If you've ever (or always) dreamed of marrying the *beit midrash* (study hall) with the artists' studio, this beautiful book is for you. It will introduce you to a wonderful method and a remarkable teacher."
— **Rabbi Shai Held**, author of *Judaism Is About Love: Recovering the Heart of Jewish Life*

"How blessed we are to find a sacred path that fuses creativity, wisdom, and connection across the ages. And how blessed among the blessed that we now have a master teacher, Rabbi Adina Allen, to translate that wisdom into words to nurture our souls, to open our creative possibilities, and to fuse the personal and the communal with the spiritual and the artistic."
— **Rabbi Dr. Bradley Shavit Artson**, Roslyn and Abner Goldstine Dean's Chair and Professor of Philosophy at American Jewish University

"*The Place of All Possibility* expands the field of the arts from a discipline for the few to a spiritual practice for all. Rabbi Adina Allen makes explicit what has always been true in Jewish culture: that imagination is part of the process of understanding Torah, and that creativity itself is sacred. She reminds us that if we engage Torah not just through intellectual learning but through art-making, it becomes not a rigid text but a succession of fluid interpretations — enabling us to connect with it more deeply and freely. Rabbi Allen's methodology, of bringing people together with sacred stories and offering them a framework for artistic response, is an important innovation in contemporary Jewish life. This book passionately shares that innovation with us all, inviting us to find the sacred flow."
— **Rabbi Jill Hammer**, PhD, author of *Undertorah: An Earth-Based Kabbalah of Dreams*

"Rabbi Allen explores in her stimulating debut the 'immense potential of creativity' to cast 'ancient Jewish wisdom' in a new light ... Through a clever mix of artistic exercises and rabbinic wisdom, Allen encourages readers to 'peel back layers of what we think we know' to construct new understandings of their faith and themselves. It's a unique and invigorating lens on Judaism."
— ***Publishers Weekly***

The Place of All Possibility

The Place of All Possibility

Cultivating Creativity Through Ancient Jewish Wisdom

Adina Allen

Ayin Press

This book was made possible through the generous support of the
Opaline Fund, Anne Germanacos, The Covenant Foundation, and
Lippman Kanfer Foundation for Living Torah. We are grateful for
their commitment to the transformative power of creative work,
and to amplifying a polyphony of voices from within and beyond
the Jewish world.

Cover design by Gabriel Melcher
Book design and typesetting by Cem Eskinazi

Typeset in Fedra Serif designed by Peter Biľak
with Bahman Eslami, Kristyan Sarkis, Khajag Apelian, Gayaneh Bagdasarya,
Panagiotis Haratzopoulos & Michal Saha.
Released by Netherlands-based foundry Typotheque in 2003

Printed in the USA

First Edition
Second Printing

Ayin Press
Brooklyn, New York
www.ayinpress.org
info@ayinpress.org

Distributed by Publishers Group West, an Ingram brand

ISBN (paperback): 978-1-961814-03-5
ISBN (e-book): 978-1-961814-04-2

Library of Congress Control Number: 2024933276

Ayin Press books may be purchased at a discounted rate by
wholesalers, booksellers, book clubs, schools, universities,
synagogues, community organizations, and other institutions buying in bulk. For more information, please email
info@ayinpress.org.

Follow us on Facebook, Instagram, or Twitter @AyinPress.

For more resources related to *The Place of All Possibility* visit
www.theplaceofallpossibilitybook.com.

The Place of All Possibility

To my mom, Pat B. Allen, for everything.

Welcome

Welcome! However you found your way, I'm so glad you're here.

I wrote this book with the intention of opening up and making accessible the depth and richness that I have found in ancient Jewish wisdom for those of all backgrounds and beliefs. You don't have to be Jewish to use this book. Whoever you are—whether you are Jewish or not, whether you believe in God or not—you are invited, you are welcome, you are needed. Rather than being about "belief"—some abstract idea that we hold to be true—this book is about experience, particularly the experience of creativity that connects us to something deep within and beyond us. Whether we subscribe to a specific spiritual or religious tradition, or none at all, that palpable experience of presence, of partnership, of something numinous and sacred, is waiting to receive each one of us if we choose to become familiar with it.

Throughout this book, I speak often of "God." I know that this word has come to be used in so many different ways, many of which have caused harm. When I use this word, I am referring to the ineffable, enlivening, animating force that flows through everyone and everything. In addition to "God," I use many different words to refer to this force, including the Divine, Source, and YHVH (the English representation of the Hebrew name, sometimes called the tetragrammaton, that is considered unpronounceable in the Jewish tradition). Throughout the book when you come across any God language that doesn't work for you, please feel encouraged to substitute any other word that connects you to something bigger and beyond yourself. Try Spirit, the Universe, or Creativity, for example.

My deepest prayer is that this book will be a portal into the ancient and the sacred that can support and inspire all of us to blow our hearts wide open, to unlock new potential for our lives. In reading and reimagining ancient Jewish wisdom, may we breathe new life into these time-honored words so that they can be not only relevant but revitalizing. May this book serve as a bridge between the stories of the past and the stories of today so that, with love, determination, and a sense of humility and hope, we might write the stories of our collective future. May the words on these pages serve as a conceptual and practical starting point as we make our way to the place of all possibility—available to us all, in any moment, right here, right now. And, together, may we imagine and create a world of compassion, creativity and care for all.

Introduction

I grew up in an art studio. From an early age, my mother gave
me a paintbrush and pen as tools to understand myself
and the world around me. As the daughter of well-known art
therapist Pat B. Allen, throughout my childhood and adoles-
cence, I found in the studio a kind of sanctuary: a place where
I could work alongside others, bringing all the raw, messy,
in-process parts of myself, and where I could seek (and find)
insight, vision, and inspiration. I lived amid my mother's
images, many of which were evocative and unusual, and I
was fully supported to make whatever I felt moved to create.
I felt held, and seen, and whole in the open-ended creative
process that she introduced me to. These early experiences
were electrifying and energizing in a unique and powerful way,
catalyzing a quest for the source of their power and insight:
I wanted to understand the mysteries of creativity, to know
the origins of the intuition and visions that came to me while
I was working in the studio.

Eventually, and somewhat unexpectedly, this yearning
led me on a path to become a rabbi. Through six years of study
in rabbinical school, I deepened my understanding of Judaism
and my own relationship with the Divine. I became immersed
in traditional Jewish practice and study, which opened my
eyes to the richness of Jewish tradition and to the wisdom of
ancestors who had wrestled with questions both mundane
and cosmic—gifting me not only some answers but, perhaps

more importantly, sturdy and reliable frameworks through which to ask my own questions.

While I was growing up, the art studio had been my sanctuary; now I discovered a new sanctuary in the *beit midrash*. Often translated as a "study hall," the *beit midrash* is a space set aside for Jewish learning. Yet, this phrase (like so many others we will explore throughout the book) allows for multiple interpretations, each of which invites new possibilities. *Beit midrash* refers not only to a space, but also to a sacred process of learning and exploration. The word "midrash" comes from the verb *lidrosh*, meaning to seek or inquire. (It is also the name of a type of Jewish interpretive text, generated by this process of inquiry, called a midrash.) Unlike the quiet, solitary learning done in a secular library, in a *beit midrash*, one learns Jewish sacred texts with a *chavruta*—a study partner—in a dynamic, conversational give-and-take, collaboratively puzzling through the words on the page. In rabbinical school, alongside our classmates, my *chavruta* and I spent day after day studying the impassioned argumentation, fantastical stories, and grammatical explanations of early sages and rabbis. Dating back to ancient times, these discourses were recorded in the thick, gold-embossed books that lined the walls of our *beit midrash*, a collective conversation across multiple generations.

Upon induction into this sprawling world of words, our teachers in rabbinical school gave us a clear charge: it is upon you not only to study the scholars that came before you, but also to generate your own creative interpretations of Torah (a word that can encapsulate a broad swath of Jewish sacred texts, as I'll discuss further on). In other words, we were not only to learn from the ancient commentators—we were to become the commentators of today, and to invite our students and congregations to do the same. Embedded in this charge was the gem of wisdom that has fueled Judaism's continual creative evolution across millenia: the tradition must be renewed in the minds, hearts, and hands of each generation in order to meet the unique circumstances and challenges

it faces. The practice of studying ancient Jewish wisdom, which
I had thought was primarily about tradition and preservation,
turned out to be a creative process of its own. I wondered:
Could the creative process of the beit midrash *join the creative process
of the studio, providing a new pathway for a collective project of renewal
and relevance in our times*? "Yes, yes, yes!" I intuitively answered.
But how?

In the *beit midrash*, I learned the techniques that the
rabbis had developed to draw new meaning out of ancient text:
wordplay, gematria,[1] and cross-references that linked diverse
passages from the vast canon of Jewish sacred literature
to discover new understandings and sometimes surprising
connections. While these interpretive techniques allowed the
rabbis to continually, and creatively, renew the tradition and
gain insight into the challenges of their time, these practices
remained highly specialized — ensuring not only the continua-
tion of the tradition but also the primacy of the rabbi as expert.
For everyone to be invited into this project in a meaningful
way, new tools were needed.

In an attempt to answer the question of how we, in our
own way, could become the commentators of today, I began
to reflect on my early experiences in the studio — both the one
in my house growing up, and the public art studios my mom
founded and ran, where I spent much of my childhood.[2] These
studios, which used a method called the Open Studio Process,
were created with the express purpose of supporting the artist
in everyone and centering the expertise of each person in
their process of creation and self-discovery. In the *beit midrash*,
we studied Torah on the level of the intellect; as much as
I reveled in this approach, over time, I had a desire to engage

---

1 Gematria is the practice of assigning a numerical value to a Hebrew name, word,
   or phrase based on the numerical value of each Hebrew letter in it (which, much
   like Roman numerals, doubled as numbers before Arabic numerals were adopted)
   and interpreting another layer of meaning through that number.
2 The Open Studio Project, founded in Chicago in 1991 by Dayna Block, Deborah Gadiel,
   and Pat B. Allen.

more of myself in this practice—not just my intellectual mind, but my heart, my intuition and imagination, my emotions, my own story. As a rabbi, I wanted to find a way for each person to be able to bring their full selves into this dance of interpretative possibilities. I wanted to feel in the *beit midrash* the way I felt in the studio—alive, alert, illuminated, in tune—and I wanted this not just for myself, but for everyone.

As I deepened my practice of Torah study and had the opportunity to learn with many *chavrutot* (learning partners) from a variety of backgrounds, ages, and identities, I came to understand the richness that this diversity offers. Each one of us has access to unique perspectives—ways of understanding the world that emerge from our life experience and the particularity of who we are—and this uniqueness is among our greatest gifts. I felt more and more that if we could bring these unique perspectives and experiences to the text, we would be able to generate energizing, exciting, and useful new insights. Yet, I also experienced the many ways that a purely cerebral approach to the text, with a narrow focus on grammar and encyclopedic knowledge, can short-circuit our deeper learning, obstructing the primordial power of these texts to activate that authentic, vital place within us, where new meanings are born.

And so, together with like-minded colleagues and teachers, I began to experiment. I played with bringing together the creative process I had been immersed in growing up with the dynamic study of sacred texts I was learning in rabbinical school. I felt the dynamism and depth of insight that art-making, employed as a self-reflective method of inquiry, brought to the experience of learning Torah, and heard the excitement from others at the prospect of engaging in text study with their full selves. As the method developed, and as my passion for this approach grew, I began leading classes and workshops beyond the walls of our *beit midrash*. After many years of exploration and refinement, I gave this methodology a name, one that called back to my mother's work: the Jewish Studio Process. This methodology speaks to the charge my teachers originally gave me and my classmates: to cultivate the insights and the wisdom that each of us (and our whole world) needs today, and to make this process accessible to anyone and everyone who desires to engage.

The Jewish Studio Process

After graduating from rabbinical school, I began dreaming of ways to bring this methodology more fully into the world. In 2015, in collaboration with my spouse, I founded Jewish Studio Project (JSP). Now a national nonprofit, our mission is to cultivate creativity as a Jewish practice for spiritual connection and social transformation. At the core of what we do is our methodology, the Jewish Studio Process. Bringing together creative interpretive practices from the *beit midrash* with art therapy studio techniques, the Jewish Studio Process is a practice that allows each of us — regardless of our familiarity with Jewish sacred text, or perceived artistic talent — to discover, and add our own voice to, the ongoing chain of interpretation by investigating how the text speaks to and through our own lives.

As I gained more experience facilitating this process for others, and incorporating it into my own life, I began to understand the immense potential of creativity as a gateway to deeper spirituality, personal growth, and even social and political imagination. Along the way, I also encountered many obstacles to experiencing or accessing creativity among participants, most notably the ways that so many of us are cut off from this inherent source of vitality and joy. Over time, the Jewish Studio Process became not only a practice for interpreting and reimagining sacred text, but also a pastoral intervention to support people in finding ways to gently and tenderly reach towards an essential part of themselves that they had lost access to: their inherent creativity. In this book, I will lead you through the core principles of this process and provide guidance for how to practice it yourself.

The Torah of Creativity

The Jewish Studio Process is rooted in what I call the "Torah of Creativity." Drawn from ancient Jewish wisdom, the Torah of Creativity is a paradigm in which our engagement with Jewish sacred texts is understood as an opportunity to discover and access the vitality that exists within and all around us, even in the most difficult of times. While it is easy to become overwhelmed by the unpredictability of life, and the chaos and loss we encounter in the world, the Torah of Creativity grounds us in the understanding that within rupture are embedded the seeds of renewal. No matter what we are experiencing or struggling with, the Torah of Creativity invites us to ask these sacred texts to support and guide us, to rouse our imagination and inspire us, to trouble our assumptions and transform our aspirations, to open the aperture of our viewpoint and to expand our hearts. In this way, the Torah of Creativity helps us remain awake to the world as it is—in all its beauty and brokenness—and stirs within us the courage to envision and call forth the future that is waiting to be born.

What you'll find in this book

This is a guidebook to the core principles of the Torah of Creativity, and an introduction to the Jewish Studio Process. In these pages, I offer an approach that can help you unlock and amplify your own creativity and meaningfully engage ancient Jewish wisdom on your own terms. My hope is that this book will support you in deepening (or starting!) a creative practice, in developing your ability to access and appreciate the depths of Torah, and in opening new pathways into the place of all possibility.

The first part of this book takes a deep dive into the concepts of both "Torah" and "creativity," exploring the many contours and connections that live inside and between these terms. I'll start with a focus on the creativity inherent in Torah, grounding in an expansive definition of all that Torah can mean. Then, I'll explore the nature of creativity itself, and dive into the Torah of Creativity, investigating the power and potential this approach holds in our lives. Building upon these deeper understandings of Torah and creativity, I'll then take you through the steps of the Jewish Studio Process, and offer practical guidance and exercises for how you can apply this approach to sacred text and to your life.

The second part of this book moves through five core principles, five pathways drawn from ancient Jewish wisdom that can support and guide your creative process. Each pathway is defined by an enigmatic Hebrew phrase that we'll unpack together to excavate insights and wisdom to support your creative journey. At the end of each chapter, there are practice exercises that allow you to experience these concepts in action.

A note on translation

There are many Hebrew phrases quoted throughout this book. Some are lines of biblical text, some are from other Jewish sacred sources. Many translations used are my own, but they are informed by colleagues, teachers, and community members with whom I've explored these lines over the years. I have also drawn from and adapted existing translations — notably, the 1985 JPS *Hebrew-English Tanakh* for biblical passages; Sefaria community translations for various midrashic sources; Rabbi Avraham Greenbaum's translations for excerpts of Rabbi Nachman of Breslov's *Chayei Moharan*; John T. Townsend's translations for passages from Midrash Tanchuma; Daniel C. Matt's translations for passages from the Zohar; and for Talmudic excerpts, the William Davidson Talmud on Sefaria (featuring translations by Rabbi Adin Even-Israel Steinsaltz). Often my translations are similar to traditional understandings of a verse; other times, the translations I offer are a radical departure from the traditional reading. In my own practice,

I hold all of these translations together — the ones I've learned from my teachers, the ones I've found in traditional sources, the ones I have created in my own process — knowing that there are always multiple ways to translate a verse, and that I will need to call on different translations at different moments, depending on what I'm seeking (or what is seeking me). The act of translation is a process of interpretation. For me, this is what makes Torah infinitely generative and exciting as a resource for ongoing learning and discovery. I hope you find it so, too!

A note on the Hebrew language

In writing this book for an audience that includes both those familiar and those unfamiliar with Hebrew, I felt it was important to include the original Hebrew, along with the English transliteration, rather than just offer my own translation of a word or phrase. Hebrew is a rich and multifaceted language, in which each word often contains within it many possible meanings. As a Semitic language, most words are derived from three-letter "roots" with specific conceptual, symbolic, or grammatical associations. Throughout the book you will see mention of such roots, which open up the possibilities of various meanings within a particular word, phrase, or verse.

For those of you who are familiar with Hebrew, I wanted to offer you the opportunity to see the text in its original form so that you might play with your own interpretations and understandings, rather than just take mine as authoritative. Perhaps because Hebrew is an ancient language, I experience its words as containing mystery and magic beyond their strictly semantic dimension. For those of you who are new to Hebrew, I hope the inclusion of the original sources provides you with an opportunity to see the form of the letters on the page, and with the help of the transliteration and translation, to feel the power of these words and know that you are in touch with the source from which these lines came.

A blessing for the journey

Ancient Jewish wisdom teaches that blessings are a way to declare the sacredness of the task we are about to engage in, and to invite something bigger and beyond ourselves to guide and support us; they help to focus our energy and align our spirit. In Jewish tradition, the ancient rabbis codified blessings for countless daily acts—waking up in the morning, washing hands, eating food, studying Torah—but, as a participant in a workshop once pointed out to me, there was no such blessing for the act of creation.[3] So, building on the formula of traditional Jewish blessings, I created a Blessing for Creativity. Taking ideas and phrases from Jewish liturgy and weaving them together, this contemporary blessing connects our creativity to divine creativity and sanctifies our creative work as being in partnership with God in the ongoing work of creation.

ברוך אתה ה' מקור החיים שברא אותנו בצלמו
ומזמין אותנו לחדש בכל יום תמיד מעשה בראשית.
ברוך אתה ה' יוצר אותנו יצירתיים.

Baruch Atah Adonai, Mekor haChayim, shebara otanu betzalmo,
umazmeen otanu lechadeish bekhol yom tamid ma'aseh beresheit.
Baruch Atah Adonai, Yotzer otanu yetziratim.

BLESSED ARE YOU, SOURCE OF LIFE, WHO CREATED US IN YOUR IMAGE
AND INVITES US DAILY TO RENEW THE WORK OF CREATION.
BLESSED ARE YOU WHO CREATED US CREATIVE.

---

3 With gratitude to Yisrael Chai Neviah-Kogut for prompting the creation of this blessing.

A TORAH OF CREATIVITY

Creativity as Torah

When I was young, I was taught that there was one foundational prayer, composed of six Hebrew words, that encapsulated all of Judaism: *Shema Yisrael Adonai Eloheinu Adonai Echad*.
Three times a day, we were to recite these words—in morning
and evening prayers and when we got into bed to go to sleep,
making them the last words we said at the end of each day.
As a kid with big questions about the world, and some anxiety
about my own life, the practice of saying these six words
grounded me. I connected to the feel of the Hebrew in my
mouth, to the intergenerational weight of this practice, the
mantra-like quality of returning to the same six words again
and again. But every time I'd hear these words translated into
English, I'd grimace: "Hear O Israel, the Lord is our God, the
Lord is One." This, I was taught, was "the watchword of our
faith," our declaration of fidelity to a monotheistic God who
was also "our Lord." Though I tried to rally myself behind the
cause, none of these meanings felt particularly alive to me.
Yet, when it was just me with the resonance of the Hebrew words,
they felt powerful and important. It wasn't until decades later,
as my own facility with Hebrew developed, and as I encountered other interpretations[1] that opened up new meanings
of this prayer, that I began to sense the profound power and
ever-unfolding possibilities encoded in these ancient words.

---

1   With gratitude to Rabbi Michael Lerner and Rabbi Arthur Waskow, among others.

This prayer is called the Shema, after its first word. **Shema** means "hear," but within that word is also a deeper call to listen—to attune our senses and open our awareness, to make ourselves available to receive. **Yisrael** means Israel (as in, the Jewish people), but this word can also be broken down into two words: *"isra,"* one who struggles, and *"El,"* God. In this way, *Yisrael* can also be translated as "God-wrestler": all those who grapple with a force that is both deep within and far beyond ourselves. **Adonai** means "lord" or "master," but is a stand-in for what is actually written in the Hebrew text— the unpronounceable name of God. Within the four letters that make up God's unpronounceable name are all three tenses of the verb "to be"—is, was, and will be—revealing God's eternal presence throughout all time. **Eloheinu** is the possessive expression ("our") of another word for "God," declaring that this infinite source of transformation and becoming, the Source of all life that animates creation, is what we are referring to when we speak of "God." Lastly, **echad** means "one." This could be, as I had been taught, an assertion of the singularity of "one God," as opposed to many Gods; but within that word is also "oneness," or unity—another way of saying that all life is ultimately woven together and sacred.

Suddenly what had been translated for generations as "our Lord" melted away into the mystery and beauty of a power that cannot be named or pinned down. And "one" became a force that flowed through all, alerting us to the interconnection and interpenetration of all life. What had been words addressed only to Jews now became words addressed to any and all people who struggle with meaning and purpose in this world, and who wrestle with the mystery of what it is to be alive. And what had once sounded like a proclamation (hear ye, hear ye!) unfolded into an invitation to slow down, open up, and deeply listen.

This transformation took time. I had to carry these words around with me for many years until I had the tools to better decipher them. As I gained more fluency, I learned to sit with these words and unpack them letter by letter until they revealed their magic to me. I also had to contend with myself and all my doubts and insecurities in order to pursue something that called to me, even when the message of that call was unclear. Uncovering the layers of the Shema piqued my curiosity. If these six seemingly simple words of Torah contained so much potential for radical reinterpretation and emergent beauty, what was waiting for me in the rest of the Torah? And how might I be able to uncover it?

An invitation to excavation

In her book *Pentimento*, author and playwright Lillian Hellman describes a phenomenon that often occurs when we return to a piece of art we once worked on after much time has passed: "Old paint on a canvas, as it ages, sometimes becomes transparent. When that happens it is possible, in some pictures, to see the original lines: a tree will show through a woman's dress, a child makes way for a dog, a large boat is no longer on an open sea."[2] Hellman speaks of the way the aging paint allows for older layers to show through, offering an opportunity to see, in her words, "what was there for me once, what is there for me now."

Like the painting Hellman describes, Torah, too, is a work in process. Layers and layers of interpretation have been added to it over time, according to the needs, desires, fears, and longings of those who devoted their lives to making meaning out of these sacred words. Some layers add to the beauty and power of the overall piece, strokes and shapes that bring the picture more clearly and compellingly into focus. And some, like the English translation of the Shema I was taught as a child, accrue like varnish, making the painting hard and impenetrable, obscuring the softness and fluidity underneath.

2   Lillian Hellman, *Pentimento* (Boston: Little, Brown and Company, 2000), 3.

Each one of us is invited into this process of excavation, of peeling back layers of what we have been taught or what we think we know, and seeing, as Hellman writes, what is there for us now. And each of us is called to our creativity — to bring our brush back to the canvas anew, reencountering and reworking the stories, ideas, and images that lie at the very foundation of who we are and who we could be.

An infinitely renewable resource

"Torah" can mean different things to different people. For many, it may simply be synonymous with the "Hebrew Bible," or what some call the "Old Testament." However, "Torah" is a Hebrew word and in Jewish tradition, each Hebrew word is like a text in and of itself, containing multiple meanings. But before we explore the many, varied definitions and associations contained within "Torah," it may be grounding to understand how Jewish people relate to the actual Torah scroll, the ritual object, in a communal setting.

For some, the word "Torah" evokes an image of a scroll that is dressed in velvet cloth and silver finery and stored in the ark in the synagogue. In Hebrew, the ark is called the *aron kodesh*, which literally translates as "holy cabinet," and it is regarded as the holiest place in any Jewish house of worship. If you've ever been to synagogue for the ritual of communal Torah reading (e.g., on Shabbat or a holiday, or maybe for a friend's *b'mitzvah*), you've seen the pomp and circumstance that accompanies this part of the service. First, the ark is opened, the congregation rises, the Torah is removed, held close, sung about, gazed upon, paraded around, kissed, undressed, carefully set down, and scrolled to the place where the day's reading begins. Then it is read from with a beautiful, ornamental *yad*, or "hand," that follows the words on the page so that our own hands don't touch (and potentially tarnish) the scroll. The words are chanted aloud in a special "trope" (melody) that the reader has to learn before the public reading, since there are neither markings for trope, nor vowels, in the scroll itself.[3]

This elaborate choreography experientially conveys the idea that engaging with Torah is something special and sacred. The Torah scroll is kept in a holy place and reading the text requires a great deal of ritual and special skill in order to do it properly. However, while all of this ritual may increase one's reverence, it can also make the Torah feel distant—kept alone in the ark, only to be seen and read from on special occasions, and only then by those with the knowledge and skill to do the reading. And yet, this ceremony is also a way of communally investing Torah with power and potency—of saying, "What is in this scroll is special." In the way that the person who removes the Torah from the ark physically feels the weight of the Torah in their arms, we affirm the weightiness of these words of Torah that we've inherited. In the way that the person who holds the Torah up against their chest, with one hand underneath to support it, as one might hold an infant, we connect to the preciousness of the task that we, today's readers, have been given. In the way that the Torah is paraded around the congregation, so that every member of the community has a chance to reach out and touch the scroll, and then brings their fingers to their lips in a kiss, we affirm the potential for each and every person's unique connection to this sacred text, reminding ourselves of the possibilities for tender intimacy between us and these ancient words. All of these rituals ground the public reading of Torah in joy, love, and the knowledge that each and every person has their own unique relationship to and perspective on what is being read. Torah is an infinitely renewable resource, bringing us face-to-face with the Divine—in the text, in the world, in ourselves, and in each other.

---

3   In Hebrew, vowels are small dots and dashes under consonants that tell the reader how to pronounce the word.

A great voice speaks

In the wider context of Jewish culture, outside of the ritual use of the Torah scroll in a synagogue, the word "Torah" can refer to many things. In addition to the sacred text of the Chumash (commonly known as the Five Books of Moses: Genesis, Exodus, Leviticus, Numbers, and Deuteronomy), "Torah" can also refer to the entire canon of Jewish tradition, including both the Written Torah (the Chumash, Prophets, and Writings, collectively known as the Tanakh) and the Oral Torah (the collections of commentaries from the ancient through the early medieval periods that expound on the Written Torah, including the Talmud, collections of midrash, and others).[4] One might rightly ask: Why is it called the Oral Torah if it's a collection of writings? This was one of the difficult innovations following the destruction of the Second Temple, when commentaries that had previously been passed down from teacher to student as oral teachings were written down by the early rabbis so that they could be preserved in the midst of massive political and social upheaval. The decision to write down the Oral Torah went against explicit halacha (Jewish law) at the time, but it was deemed necessary in response to the chaos and uncertainty of occupation and dispersal. To write down what had, for generations, only been taught face-to-face, in some ways limited the fluid, constantly evolving nature of these stories and teachings. But this dynamic and conversational quality was retained in the style of study — which centered inquiry, debate, and innovation — that became the norm for Jewish learning in the *beit midrash*.

Even more expansively, and central to our explorations here, "Torah" can also refer to the unique insights, interpretations, and teachings that any individual might offer. For instance, in seeking your wisdom or viewpoint on a particular

---

4   A midrash is a creative interpretation in the form of extratextual narrative, something like ancient "fan fiction." These midrashim (the plural form of "midrash") were passed down as oral teachings before being compiled in books.

issue, I might ask, "What's your Torah on this?" In this way, "Torah" paradoxically refers to the "fixed" words in the scroll— and to each of our own insights and interpretations that are constantly coming forth. Torah is both written and spoken, ancient and modern, codified and ever-emergent. It can be both the isolated work of experts, as well as the communal practice of lay people with a spectrum of backgrounds, identities, and perspectives. And it can be *your* Torah—your insight, emerging from the intersection of your lived experience, your imagination, and the sacred text.

This creative tension of Torah, referring to something both ancient and new, is embedded in the text of the Torah itself. In the book of Deuteronomy, as Moses nears the end of his life, he reflects on the journey he and the Israelite people have been on. He recounts the experience of collective revelation at Mount Sinai, that soul-shaking moment when God's thunderous voice spoke. When Moses recalls this prophetic experience, he describes God's voice as *"kol gadol velo yasaf."*[5] The phrase *"kol gadol"* can be translated as "great voice," and the phrase *"velo yasaf"* is traditionally translated as "and no more." (The word *"lo"* is a negative, meaning "did not," and *"yasaf,"* from the Hebrew root *yud-samech-fei*, means "to increase, add, or repeat.") So, one traditional translation of this line is: "A great voice spoke and did not speak more [after that]." Meaning, after this singular transmission, direct revelation ceased.

However, because the Torah scroll contains no vowels, one can read the phrase *"velo yasaf"* differently. The ancient rabbis put forth the possibility that *"yasaf"* derived from another root, *samech-vav-fei*, meaning "end," from which they then derive the meaning "to stop or cease." This completely changes the meaning of the verse. In this reading, *"velo yasaf"* does not mean "did not increase, add, or repeat," but to the contrary, "did not cease." The line as a whole can then be read: "A great voice spoke these words and never stopped [speaking]."

---

5   Deuteronomy 5:19.

The rabbis' radical reinterpretation inverts the plain meaning of the verse, stating emphatically: "A great voice spoke and never ceased!" We might interpret this to say: yes, Torah was given in that particular moment of revelation on Sinai—*and* from that point on, in every generation that followed, the divine voice continues to speak and reveal new Torah. In the Jewish tradition, rather than one interpretation replacing the other, *both* interpretations are kept, even (or especially!) when they are contradictory. The Torah, then, is both what was spoken during the revelation on Mount Sinai *and also* what is constantly being revealed in every moment, whenever we open ourselves to listen to the wisdom deep within us and to the knowledge born from our lived experience. In this way, Torah is an ancient inheritance that is being continually regenerated through a never-ending conversation between Creator and creation.

Return to the root

Let's explore the deeper meanings of the word "Torah," to glean some insights about how we can connect our own lives with concepts and associations that can often feel exclusively lofty or only particular to Jewish tradition. Etymologically, the word "Torah," commonly translated as "instruction" or "law," comes from the Hebrew root *yud-resh-hei*. This root is shared by many words, including "*moreh*" (teacher) and "*lirot*" (to cast or shoot), linking their individual meanings in an etymological web of shared significance.[6] Some rabbis also postulate that the root of Torah is *hei-resh-hei*, the root of the word "*horim*," parents—

---

6   With gratitude to Rabbi Sharon Cohen Anisfeld for her beautiful introduction to Torah and the *beit midrash* offered at JSP's inaugural Studio Immersive, from which this section is drawn.

yet another iterative meaning that opens up possibilities for how we understand Torah.[7]

Drawing from the word "*horim*," we might imagine Torah as playing a parenting role in our lives—educating us in the values, morals, beliefs, and practices to help us live a good life. Torah can also act in the role of a parent to whom we bring our struggles, longings, and questions, as we seek solace, wisdom, and direction. Drawing from the word "*moreh*," Torah can play the role of teacher by helping us learn about ourselves and the world. This might mean looking for the literal laws by which to live, but that is only one kind of instruction; another kind of teaching helps us better understand ourselves—our own innate wisdom and deep knowing. In this sense, Torah can be a teacher the same way we might imagine a Rorschach inkblot to be a "teacher": we come to it with what we have, and we see in it what we need. Perhaps a particular word jumps out at us with a spark of inspiration, or our reaction to a disturbing passage helps clarify something important for us, or a line we've read numerous times before suddenly reveals new levels of meaning.

Connecting to Torah as both parent and teacher underscores the ways in which engaging with Torah is relational. We bring who we are to the text and the text offers back something of meaning to us. Our authentic engagement with the text has the power not only to change us, but, I believe, to change the text. This isn't to say that the words themselves are altered or rewritten. Rather, through our active interpretation, the text is revitalized, revealing what had been present but previously concealed within it—and within us. The words are given permission to take on entirely new meanings, beyond what had previously been apparent or accepted. The verses become infused with new wisdom that arises within each of us when we engage authentically with what is on the page.

---

7   Rav Samson Raphael Hirsch makes this argument in his commentary on Genesis 16:5, noting that to teach is to "plant a spiritual seed in someone." See Mitchell First, "What Is the Root of the Word 'Torah'?," *Jewish Link*, June 6, 2019.

Then there is the third constellation of meaning drawn from the root *yud-resh-hei* — "*lirot*": to throw, cast, or shoot (as with an arrow). This meaning spins off into many words in ancient and modern Hebrew, but connecting all of them is a sense of active directionality. To shoot or cast is to look to a certain point and extend your efforts in that direction. In the context of learning Torah, this directionality is about being open to the authenticity of your desire — the question, longing, or need you bring to the text — and the vulnerability of not knowing where you'll end up. It is imaginative and aspirational. To shoot an arrow requires tension — pulling the arrow back against the bow's string, and releasing, removing your hand from the string so that the arrow can fly. Engaging in Torah requires this dynamic, as well. There is a nuanced balance between tension and release: the active intellectual engagement and wrestling with the text and the opening up to something beyond your rational mind to allow something you don't yet know or understand to come through. There is both the desire to end up at a certain place — to glean wisdom and understanding — and the surprise of what journey the arrow of our learning takes once it is released from our grip. Torah is thus a process that aims towards a desired destination, yet the path is unknown. Each of us come to Torah with our own yearnings, questions, and needs. In our learning, each of us gets to ask: What is it that we are aiming for? What is it that we seek? Is it greater clarity? Heart-opening? Guidance? Connection? In engaging with sacred text, our longings point us in a direction; we then release our expectations and open to what rises to meet us.

The Tree of Life

Stories about the origin of the Torah reveal further guidance and insight about what exactly Torah is and how we might relate to it. In Jewish tradition, the primary metaphor for accessing Torah has been that of going up, or ascending. Moses receives the Torah from God at the top of Mount Sinai.[8] Jewish practice evokes Moses's journey whenever a person reads aloud from the Torah scroll to a congregation: this is referred to as an *aliyah*, literally an "ascent." While it is beautiful to imagine God speaking directly to Moses atop the mountain, this narrative of transcendent revelation presents serious ethical limits and calls out to be reimagined for our day.

In the revelation at Mount Sinai, Moses goes up the mountain in order to receive Torah from God, but he is not the only one to make this ascent. In fact, there are multiple trips up and down the mountain described in the text, taken not only by Moses, but by various people: seventy elders, Moses's brother Aaron, Aaron's sons Nadav and Avihu, and others. Ultimately though, it is only Moses who reaches the peak of the mountain and has a direct encounter with God.

That's the thing about mountains—the higher you go, the less room there is. In the story of Mount Sinai, it was Moses, alone, who received the Torah at the summit, while all those who had previously gone up the mountain, along with the rest of the people of Israel, remained below, only to receive God's word secondhand. The text depicts a wild and cacophonous scene leading up to the moment of revelation: the mountain is covered in smoke; there is thunder and quaking. The people, anxious and scared, ask Moses to go up the mountain on their behalf, "lest we die," they say, as they are terrified of the immediate encounter with the *mysterium tremendum*.[9] I wonder, though, what might have happened if God was not imagined to be up in the sky, and if the path to revelation wasn't up a steep mountain slope. Even had they been willing, many people wouldn't have been able to make such a journey—the very young, the very old, those with trouble walking, or those with asthma or fatigue. And at the apex, any who did make it up

---

8   Exodus 31:18.
9   Exodus 20:16.

wouldn't have been physically able to fit in the small space at the peak. When the goal is the top, there is only room for one.

With the top-down revelation at Mount Sinai mediated through Moses, the question arises of whether the people consented to receive the Torah at all. Fascinatingly, there is a midrash that depicts the moment in which God "asks" the people to accept the Torah that explores this tension—and might provide us with a more inclusive and accessible metaphor for revelation. In this midrash, God rips Mount Sinai from the Earth and holds it, menacingly, above the people, saying, "If you accept the Torah, good; if not, this will be your grave."[10] As traditionally read, the midrash portrays God as threatening the people into submission. It is a brutal scene of coercion and violence, yet within it we can find the roots of a paradigm shift in how we might think about revelation and spirituality—one that invites us to drop in and down as part of the revelatory process.

This midrash riffs on a line in the Torah that says that during the revelation at Mount Sinai, "the people stood *tachtit hahar.*"[11] Typically translated as "at the base" or "at the foot" of the mountain, the word *"tachtit"* can also mean "under." Seeking an explanation for what it could have meant for the people to be standing "under" the mountain, the rabbis imagined the mountain uprooted from its place, the summit turned upside down and held as a weapon pointed straight down at the people.[12]

However, the word *"tachtit,"* in the sense of the people being *under* the mountain, yields another possible interpretation, one which may perhaps be more life-giving and empowering than the image of God threatening the people into accepting the Torah against their will. What if instead of the mountain being held above them, we imagine that the

10 Shabbat 88a.
11 Exodus 19:17.
12 Shabbat 88a.

people stood under the mountain—while the mountain was still in place on the earth? That is, what if we took "*tachtit*" to mean "under" in the sense that in the moment of revelation, the people went underground, deep *into* the earth? What if rather than striving for the clouds, they went digging into the mud, encountering worms and mycelia and tangles of roots—the entire life-supporting network that exists underground? In other words, rather than reaching towards the heavens, what if, instead, in the moment of revelation, *adam*—we humans—were rerooting into the *adamah*, earth? Perhaps there, held in the fertile darkness deep beneath the surface, we would have been less afraid, more able to hear the voice of God and receive the sustenance that is Torah.

Rather than revelation being something that happens far away from us, up and out of reach, disconnected from the messy aliveness of life on (and of) earth, rather than there being one special person to whom Torah was given while the rest of us waited passively, in this interpretation, we can imagine Torah as all of ours, available to all when we dig deep, perhaps get a bit messy, and connect with the vitality of existence.

A beautiful extension of this earth-based perspective is found in the poetic liturgy of Jewish prayer. Here, Torah is referred to as *eitz chayim*, a "Tree of Life." In the context of a communal prayer service, every time the ritual reading of Torah is complete and the scroll is placed back in the ark, Torah is referred to by this name. To be a Tree of Life is to be ever-changing and always growing. Just as trees are fed by the energy of the sun, we feed Torah through the light of our loving attention. Just as trees move through many phases— growing branches, dropping leaves, and sprouting new buds— Torah at times may seem sparse and bare, and at other times, fruitful and fragrant. Just as we often think of trees as only what's visible aboveground, we are wise to remember that Torah is much more than what is visible on the page: it too has depths beneath the surface of the text, like the fertile darkness of the earth, and the wild places within our souls.

Rewilding revelation

Throughout traditional texts, Torah is compared not only to
a tree, but to fire, water, rain, iron, a gazelle, and more. All of
these metaphors are rooted in the more-than-human world,
in natural elements and wild animals. It is no wonder, then, that
the Torah is given in the *midbar*, the wilderness. Wilderness
is uncultivated, where human beings have not yet staked their
claim. As it says, "And God spoke to Moses in the wilderness
of Sinai."[13] A midrash on this verse asks, "Why the wilderness
of Sinai?" The rabbis answer, "Anyone who does not make
themselves ownerless like the wilderness cannot acquire the
wisdom and the Torah."[14] The Hebrew word that is translated
as "ownerless" is *"hefker."* The word appears frequently in
Jewish law, where it is commonly used to refer to ownerless
property. What does it mean to make ourselves *hefker*? Applied
metaphorically to ourselves, the midrash invites us to ask:
To whom or to what have I become beholden? What has "domes-
ticated" me and where has my wildness been tamed? In other
words, who or what "owns" me? What ideas dominate my
thinking? What habits foreclose new ways of seeing, feeling,
or being? In making ourselves *hefker*, we are renouncing,
or disentangling, ourselves from whatever "ownership" has
claimed us—advertising, dogma, ideology, our own self-
conception—and returning to a state of freedom and openness.

According to Jewish law, there are two kinds of ownerless property: (1) property that has never been owned before,
such as plants and wild animals;[15] and (2) property that has
been abandoned, or cannot be returned, and thus has ceased to
belong to its former owner.[16] The Torah of Creativity can help
us disentangle ourselves (even if only temporarily) from our
spiritual domestication and rewild ourselves. In this way

---

13 Numbers 1:1.
14 Bamidbar Rabbah 1:7.
15 Maimonides, Mishneh Torah, Zekhiyah uMattanah, 1:1–2.
16 See, for example, Babylonian Talmud, Nedarim 43a.

we then inhabit both legal categories of *hefker*: no longer belonging to our former "owners," we reclaim our connection to the undomesticated life within us—the fish and birds and flowing rivers—and to the wild nature of who we truly are.

These threads of ancient Jewish wisdom suggest that it's here, in the literal wilderness of a thousand sparkling stars, in the birdsong and bramble, that Torah is received. Among the high grasses and thick mossy trees, on the sand-swept dunes glittering under radiant blue sky, beside the babbling brook singing sweet songs to the ancient stones, we open to receive Torah, and Torah opens to receive us. It is in the wilderness, in the aliveness of the world, that Torah comes alive. When we enter into our own internal wilderness—those uncharted places within us—our preconceived ideas have space to unravel and we abandon the well-trod road of tightly held beliefs for the unkempt, unmarked path that we make by journeying. In the vast, boundless wilderness, beyond human constructs both ideological and material, beyond that which we've domes-ticated to serve our needs, Torah is truly able to blossom and become available to us. And it is when we, too, become *hefker*, like the wilderness, that we are open to all that might arise.

Resounding silence

Another beautiful expression of nature's revelatory power is found in the word *"midbar"* itself, which is etymologically related to the word *"dibur,"* meaning speech. Linking these two words, the rabbinic sages identified the wilderness as the place where we were most available to hear God's voice, and to appreciate the divine speech of creation. In other words: *the wilderness speaks*, if we would but listen. When we quiet the constant chatter in our mind, we open up a space in which we are able to hear new voices, those that speak in a language, cadence, or vocabulary that may be unfamiliar. With the understanding that Torah was given in the wilderness, we might then ask: What was it, exactly, that the people heard in that intense and wild moment when Torah was revealed? Indeed, for hundreds of years, many sages and mystics have asked this very question.

The Talmud teaches that at the moment of revelation, we received all the Torah teachings that will ever be.[17] Every book, commentary, and scroll, every word of wisdom from every generation, was revealed in that moment. Another teaching suggests that we received the entirety of the Chumash, and nothing more.[18] The Torah was given to Moses by God, and (as we say) "the rest is commentary."[19] Others focus specifically on how the messages were given that day, and by whom. According to Rabbi Yehoshua ben Levi, in that ground-shaking, heart-stopping moment, the first two of the Ten Commandments — "I am YHVH your God" and "You shall have no other gods before Me" — were communicated not via Moses but directly from God.[20] About the first commandment — "I am YHVH your God" (in Hebrew, *"Anochi YHVH Elohecha"*) — the nineteenth-century commentator Rabbi Naftali Tzvi Horowitz of Ropshicz writes, in a startling interpretation suggested by his teacher Rabbi Menachem Mendel of Rimanov, that those standing at Mount Sinai heard far less: "It is possible that at Sinai we heard nothing from the mouth of God other than the letter aleph of the first utterance '*Anochi YHVH Elohecha*,' 'I am YHWH your God.'"[21]

Aleph, the first letter of the first word in the Ten Commandments, *"anochi"* ("I am"), is also the first letter of the Hebrew alphabet. On its own, *aleph* is a silent letter until a vowel is placed beneath it. An aleph without a vowel is pure potential, an inhale that comes before speech; it is that moment of possibility before any word is uttered. In this understanding, the Torah that we received at Sinai was that of

17 Babylonian Talmud, Megillah 19b:5.

18 Pirkei Avot 1:1.

19 Rabbi Hillel famously taught: "That which is hateful to you, do not do to your neighbor. This is the entirety of Torah; the rest is commentary." Babylonian Talmud, Shabbat 31a.

20 Shir haShirim Rabbah (Vilna) 1:2.

21 Rabbi Naftali Tzvi Horowitz of Ropshicz, *Zera Kodesh*, Shavuot.

infinite potential, a pregnant pause before *everything* becomes *something*. In *God & the Big Bang*, Zohar scholar Daniel C. Matt writes, "The Aleph of revelation finds expression moment by moment."[22] The undomesticated, unvocalized *aleph* is revealed in the ownerless space of the wilderness; how it gets shaped and articulated is up to us.

As each of the texts we have explored help to elucidate, Torah is so much more than an out-of-date book or a fixed set of rigid "laws." Like a divining rod used to search for water, Torah is a powerful and sacred tool for honing in on our most pressing questions, yearnings, and intuitions. When we bring our creativity to Torah, it can lead us to jewels of wisdom and the flow of life energy that we seek in every moment, if we are open to receiving. But what does this mean, to bring our creativity to Torah?

Cultivating Torah

While "Torah" is a Hebrew word used by Jewish people to refer to our most sacred text, the impact of how we interpret the stories contained within the Torah extends far beyond the Jewish community. Though understood in different ways, and used for different purposes at different times, these stories and teachings have been and continue to be foundational for myriad cultures throughout the world, from the ancient Middle East to medieval Europe, from the American Civil Rights movement to modern art, from literary theory to new age spirituality. Whether we consider ourselves "religious" or not, we are all likely familiar with the stories of Adam and Eve, Moses on Mount Sinai, and the Exodus from Egypt. Archetypes, stories, and symbols that originate in the Torah have become ingrained in many cultural frameworks, and can

---

22 Daniel C. Matt, *God & the Big Bang: Discovering Harmony between Science & Spirituality*, 2nd ed. (Woodstock, VT: Jewish Lights Publishing, 2016), 110.

be found in everything from children's stories to protest songs, to blockbuster movies, and even Super Bowl ads.[23]

Regardless of whether we identify as atheist, spiritual, or religious (or somewhere in between), these stories have undoubtedly seeped into us on some level, often without us even being conscious of it. Even if we don't have any personal connections to them, they've shaped our society, for both good and bad, through the values and laws that have been derived from them. For example, from the Torah we get the right to a fair trial[24] and mandated days of rest[25] (hooray for the weekend!)—as well as opposition to gay rights[26] and support for capital punishment.[27] The essential point here is that the interpretations that led to these laws are not the only possible interpretations of the text. In fact, Torah has been interpreted in numerous, divergent ways for at least three thousand years, often to radically surprising ends.

Take the story of Adam and Eve. The most widespread interpretation of this story is that Eve tricked Adam into eating the forbidden fruit and was then punished by God. In this version, Eve is responsible for the expulsion from the paradisiacal Garden of Eden—and, by extension, for all the suffering we humans experience in our post-Edenic world. She is the symbol of women as cunning, manipulative, and deceitful beings who ultimately lead men (and humanity) astray. However, Jewish tradition teaches that there are "seventy faces to Torah,"[28] that is, there are countless ways to interpret and make sense of any word, line, or myth (or even letter!). While the interpretation most of us know may seem like the most obvious or straightforward way of reading the text, it often only seems that way because that is the version

---

23 Avocados From Mexico, television commercial, Super Bowl LVII, 2023.
24 See, for example, Leviticus 19:15 and Deuteronomy 16:18–19.
25 Exodus 20:8–10.
26 Leviticus 18:22.
27 Exodus 21:12.
28 Bamidbar Rabbah 13:16.

we've been taught, or the one we've heard the most, that
has been codified as "truth." However, as we have already seen
in our exploration of the moment of revelation, from the
ancient rabbis to modern-day commentators, in every generation there have been those who found other ways of reading
the text—staying true to the words but deriving different
meanings, and lifting up different lessons and values.

For example: one possible reading of this story, which
still stays true to the text, is that rather than a sinful act that
led to the downfall of humanity, Eve's eating of the apple
was a brave choice that propelled humanity forward. While God
warns Adam that if they eat of the fruit, they will die,
the snake tells Eve that is not true, she will not die, but rather
that her and Adam's "eyes will be opened."[29] Indeed, the text
mirrors this exact language after Eve and Adam eat the fruit:
"The eyes of both of them were opened."[30] Rather than being
"duped" by the snake, Eve draws on her own powers of perception; the text says she "saw that the tree was good for eating
and a delight to the eyes, and that the tree was desirable as a
source of wisdom."[31] One could argue that for humanity to
move out of an infantilized state of existence, and to allow for
moral development and the evolution of human consciousness, the fruit had to be eaten. In this reading, Eve is a heroine—
brave, wise, and resourceful, acting in collaboration with the
more-than-human world (the snake), and trusting her own
intuition and desire. Rather than negate the more widespread
interpretation of Eve, in Jewish tradition, both of these interpretations live side by side.

To be sure, given the immense harm that certain interpretations of Torah have done, it is only natural to want to defi-
nitively disprove, or erase, the perspectives we do not agree with.
This, however, goes against the ethos of Jewish textual

---

29 Genesis 3:5.
30 Genesis 3:6–7.
31 Genesis 3:6.

interpretation, which seeks to amass ever more varied under-standings of the text. Notably, the Talmud records dissenting opinions alongside accepted rulings, preserving the polyvocal-ity of rabbinical debate for future generations. Not only does this provide us with a wider and more diverse range of ideas to turn to as we, and the world, continue to change, it also main-tains the value and power of holding many things to be true at once. Rather than attempting to remove the "undesirable," or discarded, interpretations from the record, instead we are all invited to add ever-new interpretations to the discussion. Writer and mythologist Sophie Strand refers to this constant compilation of interpretation and retelling as "the compost heap" of collective meaning.[32] It is only by adding to the "heap," so to speak, that Torah (or any mythology) becomes, as Strand calls it, "good soil" from which new life can grow—and from which ever more possibilities can emerge.

---

32 "Sophie Strand on Ecological Embodiment, New Myths and Healthism // Compost Heap Wisdom," March 30, 2023, in *All That We Are*, interview by Amisha Ghadiali, podcast.

Torah as Creativity

In my home growing up, the art studio was the biggest room in our house. As a kid, whenever I was faced with a problem I couldn't figure out, like a fight with a friend or a big decision, I would go to my mom (who also happened to be an art therapist) for guidance. After hearing what I was struggling with, she would take a deep breath and respond, "Well, have you made art about it yet?" It was not usually the response that I, an anxious and angsty preteen, had been looking for; I often just wanted the adult in my life to give me a simple answer to my problems. It was only later that I understood, and was able to appreciate, the value of my mom's question. I came to realize that she was teaching me two profound truths: one, that the answers to my conundrums exist within myself; and two, that accessing creativity was a powerful way to discover what those answers might be.

No matter how annoyed or dissatisfied I was with this response, every time I took my mom's advice to "make art about it," I would invariably experience the power and medicine of creative practice and come away changed, feeling more open, clear, grounded, connected. In those days, my mom would often be in the studio alongside me, working with and through her own struggles and questions. She never trained me how to use specific materials or master a particular technique. Instead, our time in the studio was another kind of apprenticeship; watching how my mom worked with materials invited me into a particular approach to art-making and creativity. Her creative practice has always been about exploration and deep expression that lets sensation and intuition lead. I would look at the shelves of art materials—the shades of yellow, thick and buttery in the jar of paints, or the richness of the oil pastels—pick one that sparked my energy for whatever reason, and without a plan or goal, I would begin (as my mother encouraged me) by simply "making marks on the page."

Even with an art material I was excited about, oftentimes it was difficult to get started, especially if I was angry, frustrated, despondent, or lonely; if my mind was elsewhere and my stomach was in knots. At the beginning, making art almost always felt like a waste of time. "Why am I coloring?" I would ask myself, when what I *really* needed was to solve whatever problem was plaguing me. Yet, within a few minutes of mark-making, the pleasure of creating would begin to seep in, melting my resistance, or at least distracting me enough to keep going. The way two colors looked beautiful together would capture my mind, and for a minute or two, the problem would recede and something else would come to the fore: curiosity, concentration, creativity. It is not that the problem would go away, but something else would emerge: a feeling of flow and, often, even delight.

Using materials in this way gave me something to focus on while emotions swirled within me. It became an outlet for my energy and let my thinking mind relax. Like a walk in the woods, or daydreaming on the couch, this kind of creative practice, embodied and all-encompassing, gave me a chance to let thoughts come and go unbidden. Inevitably, if I stayed with it long enough, striving would give way to surrender, and loneliness would give way to feeling of presence. While engaging with this practice, I found that as I became more connected to myself, my creations began to feel like companions. Over time, I began to feel the presence of something else there with me too. I didn't have words for it at the time, but looking back, I would describe it as a feeling of flow, a sense that I was being supported by something I couldn't touch or see. Over a long, winding, and unwinding process, I have come to call this something "God." I began to understand that to "make art about it" (as my mother would say) is not just to draw a picture — it is to draw down the Divine into our midst.

The wellspring

The Talmud records a conversation between the first-century sage Rabbi Yochanan ben Zakkai and his student Rabbi Eliezer ben Hurcanus on the power and necessity of creativity, which speaks to the kind of experiences I had growing up in the studio. Seeking to be inspired by new interpretations of Torah, and acknowledging the wisdom of his student, Rabbi Yochanan says, "Eliezer, teach us one thing from the words of the wise." Rabbi Eliezer demurs, and instead says to his teacher, "Let me give you a parable: To what may I be compared? To a cistern that cannot produce more water than was put in it." Rabbi Eliezer is telling Rabbi Yochanan, basically, that he, like a cistern, is simply a vessel to hold and preserve his teacher's — Rabbi Yochanan's — wisdom (the water, in this analogy). Rabbi Yochanan replies, "No, my student. Let me give *you* a parable: To what may you be compared? To a spring. Just as when a spring begins to flow, it produces water from its own sources, so you can teach words of Torah more than were conveyed to Moses at Mount Sinai."[1] In his reply, Rabbi Yochanan seems to be saying to his student Rabbi Eliezer that the great voice that the ancient Israelites heard on Mount Sinai is still speaking. Torah, he is saying, is a wellspring bubbling inside you; let those waters flow so that we all may have a sip!

---

1 Avot deRabbi Natan, Version B, 13. As cited in Noam Zion, "Can Later Rabbinic Creativity Transcend its Origins: Moshe v. Akiva in the Talmud," Shalom Hartman Institute, June 1, 2008.

Whether we consider ourselves sage or student (or both), inside each one of us there is a bubbling spring of life-giving water. Call it God, intuition, vision—it is there within us and will remain there as long as we are alive. Sometimes it gets hidden underneath the mess of life, but whenever we are ready to uncover it, we need only to move aside the debris that has blocked its path, and we will find it there, flowing crisp and cool, nurturing and clear, a spring of vitality ready to renew us. The spring of creativity is our most potent renewable resource. It's how we stay awake to beauty and possibility amid the disarray and disappointment of life. It's how we envision new paths and work up the courage to follow them. It's how we bring forth insights that can transform barriers into thresholds, and reveal possibilities that were previously unimaginable. Creativity is a capacity that exists in everyone. It is the sparking of new energy and fresh insight; it is inspiration and imagination; it is resilience; it is the ability to move with, and through, challenge and change with openness, curiosity, and courage. As humans, we need creativity in our lives—and the world needs our creativity.

Creativity is healthy

Creativity is not just the realm of daydreaming artists, mystics, and musicians; it is also a subject of scholarly research and scientific experimentation. The science of creativity bridges various disciplines, from psychology and neuroscience, to education and business. Scientists are attempting to understand a range of issues, from what makes creativity possible from a psychological perspective, to what is actually happening in the human brain when people are "creative," to how we might actively cultivate creativity in our lives. Research into these questions is expanding as the field of creativity studies grows. The Society for the Neuroscience of Creativity lists twenty-four labs around the world that are dedicated to the research of creativity, at institutions such as Stanford, Duke, the Sorbonne, and the Technion. And yet, even for these accomplished scientific researchers, a full understanding of how creativity happens in the brain remains elusive. Dr. Anna Abraham, author of *The Neuroscience of Creativity*, writes that "we have only scratched the surface" of this topic. Part of the challenge, she explains, is that one cannot simply produce creativity in research subjects the same way one can trigger other physiological or psychological phenomena (e.g., fear, relaxation, focus).[2] It's hard to scientifically study something that cannot be consistently reproduced in a lab. Like Torah, creativity is wild and untamable, working its magic in para- doxical ways and unexpected places.

Another challenge to the study of creativity is how to define it, and then, how to measure it. There are differing opinions among scientists as to whether or not some people are inherently more creative than others — or if we all have the same capacity for creativity. There are some research psychol- ogists who argue that their findings show that people who are considered more creative than others are "wired" differently.[3] On the other hand, research in neuroplasticity[4] suggests that our brains' wiring is actually quite malleable, and that creativity itself plays a key role in maintaining this malleable bility — meaning that the more we draw on our creativity, the more our creativity grows.[5] This emerging body of research strongly resonates with my own personal and professional

2 Scott Barry Kaufman, "The Neuroscience of Creativity: A Q&A with Anna Abraham," *Scientific American*, January 4, 2019.

3 Roger Beaty, "Why Are Some People More Creative than Others?" *Scientific American*, January 16, 2018.

4 Roger E. Beaty's work has been instrumental in elaborating the framework of neuroplasticity. See Roger E. Beaty, "The Creative Brain," *Cerebrum* (January–February 2020).

5 Creativity is linked to enhanced cognitive abilities, including improved problem-solving skills, flexible thinking, and increased cognitive resilience. Creative thinking promotes the development of neural connections and stimulates cognitive growth. See Justin James Kennedy and Marlene Gonzalez, "How Neuroplasticity Affects Creativity," *Psychology Today*, updated June 13, 2023. Kennedy and Gonzalez are drawing on Beaty, "The Creative Brain."

experience: every person I work with—from those who work in "creative" professions such as artists, entrepreneurs, and designers, to those who tentatively wade into their creativity—becomes more expansive, expressive, and able to embrace the ongoing flow of their creative energy through such regular creative practice. As we'll explore in the next chapter, the Jewish Studio Process was developed to nurture and support the creative capacity in everyone.

When we think of creativity, many of us immediately think of the arts. Indeed, drawing, writing, movement, and making music can be powerful modalities for us to connect to our creativity. Susan Magsamen, the founder and director of the International Arts + Mind Lab at Johns Hopkins University School of Medicine and the codirector of the NeuroArts Blueprint with the Aspen Institute, argues that creativity is an essential ingredient in a healthy lifestyle and that making art is a powerful way to exercise and enhance our creativity. Magsamen and Ivy Ross, who co-authored the book *Your Brain on Art: How the Arts Transform Us*, explain how engaging in art-making can help us develop our creativity and enhance our well-being. They write that:

> *We are literally wired for art, and these experiences alter a complex physiological network of interconnected, neurological, and biological systems … The arts are one of the best ways to enliven these neurological systems … The bottom line is the arts positively impact every area of your life, including your physical and mental health, learning, flourishing, and community building.*[6]

In a stunning assertion based on their extensive research, the authors write that "20 minutes a day of art is as beneficial as getting enough exercise and sleep."[7] In this context,

---

6   Susan Magsamen and Ivy Ross, "Your Brain on Art: How the Arts Transform Us," *Next Big Idea Club Magazine*, April 7, 2023.
7   Magsamen and Ross, "Your Brain on Art."

making art could be anything from doodling to crafting, from journaling to singing with a group of friends. Whether done alone or together, stimulating our creativity through art-making can improve our mental and physical health while helping us find a sense of joy, expansiveness, and connection to others and to ourselves.

But creativity extends well beyond even this broad definition of "art." Dr. Ruth Richards, a psychology professor at Saybrook University and Harvard Medical School, coined the term "everyday creativity" to refer to the ways creativity can support us in our day-to-day lives.[8] Examples of such "everyday creativity" include things like caregiving, fixing your home, or designing a spreadsheet for work, all of which can activate our capacities for creative thought and problem solving. When we acknowledge and honor the creativity inherent in such everyday activities, we expand our definition of what this word means and who is considered "creative." Richards's research suggests that engaging in creative practices makes us more observant, collaborative, and brave, and less self-defensive, providing opportunities for self-reflection and self-awareness. When we are in touch with our creativity, we are in touch with the core of who we are. "It makes you more resilient, more vividly in the moment," Richards says, "and, at the same time, more connected to the world."[9] This research echoes other psychologists who have pointed out the widespread psychological and cognitive benefits of a regular creative practice.

Activating our creativity not only helps us in accomplishing needed tasks; it also can support us in navigating our days with more calm and purpose. At a time when we are facing what the US surgeon general has called an "epidemic of loneliness," and an alarmingly high rate of mental health

8 Carlin Flora, "Everyday Creativity," *Psychology Today*, November 1, 2009.
9 Flora, "Everyday Creativity."

crises among youth, creativity is more important than ever.[10] The pleasure we feel when we engage our capacity for creativity allows us to open up and soften our hard edges, and can help us see ourselves in the larger creative project of life. Studies have shown that being creative provides opportunities for cathartic release, while reducing stress, anxiety, and depression.[11] Besides reducing negative emotions, creativity invites positive experiences and strengthens our ability to cope with the difficulties of life through increasing emotional regulation, developing cognitive flexibility, and exercising our problem-solving skills. Dr. Abraham explains: "The creative mode involves turning away from the path of least resistance and venturing into the briars so to speak in an effort to forge a new path through the gray zone of the unexpected, the vague, the misleading or the unknown."[12] In short, creativity is a capacity that can help us navigate the complexity and ambiguity we encounter in the world with greater ease, imagination, and joy.

The Hungarian American psychologist Mihaly Csikszentmihalyi had a word for the subjective experience of creativity that encapsulates these feelings of ease and joy: "flow." In his groundbreaking 1990 book on creativity, *Flow: The Psychology of Optimal Experience*, he explored the state of flow experienced by people in the midst of creative engagement. In a flow state, creativity pours through us like a river whose current moves along unimpeded. Flow, for Csikszentmihalyi, is a "state in which people are so involved in an activity that nothing else seems to matter; the experience itself is so enjoyable that people will do it … for the sheer sake of doing it."[13] More recently, researchers

10 "New Surgeon General Advisory Raises Alarm about the Devastating Impact of the Epidemic of Loneliness and Isolation in the United States," US Department of Health and Human Services website, May 3, 2023.

11 Ashley Stahl, "Here's How Creativity Actually Improves Your Health," *Forbes*, July 25, 2018.

12 Kaufman, "The Neuroscience of Creativity: A Q&A with Anna Abraham."

13 Mihaly Csikszentmihalyi, *Flow: The Psychology of Optimal Experience* (New York: Harper Perennial, 1991), 4.

in creativity studies have focused on flow states specifically, and found that the state of flow induced by creative activities contributes to overall mental well-being.[14] In my own work, I've found that once we have an embodied experience of flow, it is much easier to access that state no matter what we're engaged in, whether it's in the realm of the arts, an everyday household task, a professional challenge, or a social interaction.

Taken altogether, researchers in this emerging field make the scientific case for something I have long believed based on my own personal experience and found verification of in my work with others: creativity is good for the mind, good for the soul, and good for society.

Finding our flow

All of us can likely recall times when we felt we were in a state of flow: deeply immersed in what we were doing, enlivened by the free circulation of ideas as insights or images streamed to us and through us. And most of us probably wish we could access this state, and the pleasure and generativity it brings, more easily and more often. Opening to this flow is something we can practice. And, as research in neuroplasticity suggests, I believe that the more we engage our creativity, the more easily we can access it. When we are tapped into our creativity, acting from this place of inspiration and aliveness, we can feel something beyond, and paradoxically deep within, coming through us. It is sometimes hard to tell what has been created by us and what was the work of this other force. I've often heard people say—and felt myself—that creating is itself an act of receiving. Rather than saying "I wrote this song," we might say, "That song came through me." This is another side of the idea of "flow": rather than an artist acting alone, the artist becomes a vessel through which creativity flows.

14 Stahl, "Here's How Creativity Actually Improves Your Health."

Returning to the Talmudic story of the teacher, Rabbi Yochanan, and his disciple, Rabbi Eliezer: Rabbi Eliezer saw himself as simply a receptacle for his teacher's creativity; while Rabbi Yochanan, in contrast, saw his student Eliezer as a channel for the headwaters from which he, Rabbi Yochanan, also partakes—the bountiful source from which new creativity pours forth. Using the metaphor of a spring, Rabbi Yochanan encourages his student to connect to the Source within himself, the life-giving waters of creativity. Rabbi Yochanan encourages Rabbi Eliezer in this way, I think, not only because he is committed to the growth and development of his student, but also because he knows that he himself will be enlivened and enriched by whatever creative interpretations his student offers. Nearly two thousand years before anyone studied the neuroscience of creativity, Rabbi Yochanan deeply understood the benefits of creative practice.

In truth, both Rabbi Yochanan and Rabbi Eliezer are correct. Creative interpretation—and perhaps creativity of any kind—requires us to be both cisterns and springs: opening ourselves to learn from those who have come before us while allowing our own inspiration to bubble to the surface and mix in new and unexpected ways. In a related story, after a similar exchange with Rabbi Yochanan, Rabbi Eliezer takes his teacher's invitation and sits speaking words of Torah. As he speaks, the text tells us, his face shone bright like the sun.[15] In touch with his creativity, he was aglow, lit up from the inside out. Rabbi Eliezer's face shone so bright, this midrash tells us, those around him became disoriented, unsure if it was day or night. When the student brought his full self to his practice, something magnificent happened: his insights and interpretations were so powerful that preexisting categories of night and day were confused, and the world around him was seen in a way it had never been seen before.

---

15 Pirkei deRabbi Eliezer 2:3.

This story surfaces a profound teaching: creativity is not our own genius, but rather it is a force that flows through us and connects us to our deeper selves, and to the Divine. This idea of the life-giving flow of creativity is found throughout the expansive body of ancient Jewish wisdom. In Torah, when Adam and Eve, the first human beings, are created, they are situated in the Garden of Eden. As described in Genesis, Eden was a verdant paradise of lush fruit trees, and through it, a stream flowed. This stream gently and steadily percolated through the garden, providing water, the necessary ingredient for life. The Zohar, a book of mystical commentary on the Torah, teaches that this stream symbolizes God, the animating force of the universe that flows through all of creation, and that we are the garden, watered by this divine flow.[16] Or, in the words of the writer and ecologist John Muir, the rivers flow "not past, but through us, thrilling, tingling, vibrating every fiber and cell of the substance of our bodies, making them glide and sing."[17] In the context of the Torah of Creativity, one might say: the river is creativity itself, nourishing the Tree of Life, our shared body of ancient wisdom, in the midst of the Garden, which can be understood as both our consciousness and our community. The same water that flowed through the Garden of Eden flows through you and me. Our task is to keep the channel open so that we may receive the flow of creativity and our garden may remain lush and verdant.

---

16 Melila Hellner-Eshed, *A River Flows from Eden: The Language of Mystical Experience in the Zohar*, trans. Nathan Wolski (Stanford, CA: Stanford University Press, 2009).

17 John Muir, "Mountain Thoughts," in *John of the Mountains: The Unpublished Journals of John Muir*, ed. Linnie Marsh Wolfe (Madison, WI: University of Wisconsin Press, 1979), 92.

Not just for artists

From my many years of experience facilitating workshops on
creativity for a wide range of people from diverse professions,
I have learned one thing that is essential to clarify from the
start: creativity is not the same thing as "Art." "Art" with a
capital "A" is a word we tend to associate with galleries, museums,
and the rarefied world of "artistic genius," people with special
talents or highly developed craft. Creativity, on the other hand,
is available to us all—it is a basic human capacity that does
not need to be earned. Building on Dr. Richards's idea of
"everyday creativity," we might say that creativity is the ordinary—
and extraordinary—process of noticing what's on hand and
finding magic and beauty in whatever is in front of us: a line
of text that intrigues us, a problem that perplexes us, a shape
that delights us, a task that calls to us. When we approach
what life presents us with from a place of creativity, we notice
things differently—we're less focused on outcomes, and we
become intrigued by details that might have otherwise
escaped our attention. In other words, everything becomes
an opportunity for exploration and generativity. To live from
our creativity is to find abundance in the limitations of our
life at any given moment, and to "make art about it," using
whatever tools we have at our disposal.

Here I am talking about creativity *as process.* The creative
process is a way to work with that which is overwhelming,
challenging, or unknown; a way to bring forth whatever is
needed in the moment. Each day, as we go about our lives,
there are things we encounter or experience that shock or
confuse or enchant us. As my mom writes in *Art Is a Spiritual
Path: Engaging the Sacred through the Practice of Art and Writing*,
the creative process can be a means "to enter, to play with,
to dance with, to wrestle with anything that intrigues, delights,
disturbs, or terrifies us."[18] It allows us to reflect the pain,

18 Pat B. Allen, *Art Is a Spiritual Path: Engaging the Sacred through the Practice of Art and Writing* (Boston: Shambhala Publications, 1995), 1.

strangeness, and joy of the world back to others, while also exploring, processing, and deepening our understanding of ourselves as we live through these experiences.

So many of us have internalized the limiting idea that we are not creative—and, just as hindering, the idea that creativity is frivolous, extraneous, self-indulgent, and disconnected from the very real issues we face. Even now, as an adult who has felt the rich benefits of the creative process time and again, I often find myself asking those same questions I would ask as a child when my mom would encourage me to "make art about it," only from a more "grown-up" perspective. As a spiritual leader who seeks a better world for all, the questions that now make me doubt the importance of this work sound like: *What purpose does the creative process serve when there is so much pain and suffering in the world? How can I sit here drawing pictures, or exploring my imagination, when the world is burning and people's lives are at stake?* When I'm able to sit with these questions long enough to discover what's beneath their surface, I usually find that they come from a feeling of resistance, which is often also a form of self-protection. My reticence to engage in the creative process comes from my deep knowledge that it will take me into a truth, a struggle, or a question that is begging for my attention, but that I might want to avoid. Again and again I have found that when I do choose to engage in the creative process, despite my lingering doubts and judgments, it helps me to understand and tend to this resistance with courage and care. For all of us, the creative process can help us to work through thorny issues within ourselves, open to new insights and ideas, and excavate emotions that may normally stay hidden under the surface.

We all want the world to be a better place—more just, more sustainable, more peaceful, more kind—but our stated values and aspirations often don't perfectly line up with our actions in the world. Rather than something to be ashamed of, this slippage between what we desire and what we actually do is a fertile place to explore. The creative process is uniquely suited for this task. When we access that place of creativity in ourselves, we know that we are held by and connected to a force larger than ourselves. From this place of connection we are humbled and whole, and this can help us realign our internal experience with our external selves that are active in the world. In our creative practice, our defenses can come down and the place of all possibility opens to us. In this state, whatever issues in the world call out to us do so because of an alignment with our gifts and our wounds. When we use the creative process to befriend, shift, or transform challenges in our own lives, we become more available to ways we can be in service to address the suffering of the world. To live from our creativity is to be able to discover the infinite possibilities within any challenge that life presents us. By disentangling creativity from "Art," we can forge a new relationship with our own creative potential—one that can enliven and guide us on our path through the peaks and valleys of life, love, work, and play.

And once we disentangle creativity from "Art," there is something uniquely powerful about the embodied process of art-making that helps us to unlock our inner creativity. A more open and exploratory creative practice is different than one that focuses on composing songs to be performed, or creating paintings to be hung and sold in a gallery; and yet it utilizes the same raw materials of creation—both the art materials themselves, and the chaos and void of life from which all new creations are born. This common and cosmic approach to creative practice is its own form of artistry that we can engage, develop, and deepen, regardless of the medium.

Cultivating creativity

Within Torah there are numerous stories and images that provide evocative examples of how the creative process can connect us more meaningfully to our own inner truth, to others in our community, and to the Divine. None, perhaps,

more powerfully than the story of the *mishkan*, the portable
sanctuary that God commanded the Israelites to construct
during their forty years of wandering in the wilderness
of Sinai. The sanctity of the *mishkan* came from both product
and process—the way it was created was as important as
the final creation itself.

     In the Torah, much attention is given to exactly how,
and with what materials, the *mishkan* was built. Importantly,
the construction of the *mishkan* was not a solo endeavor.
This sacred meeting place between the Divine and humans
was cocreated by the community, with contributions from
everyone. In Exodus, God gives the people a blueprint for
the structure: intricate details of measurements, materials,
color, texture, and craft. There were washing basins to be
constructed, curtains to be sewed, structures to be assembled,
tables, cherubs, arks, and menorahs to be made. Skilled
artisans, most notably two named Betzalel and Oholiav, were
key leaders in the construction process, but they were by no
means the only ones. Throughout the descriptions of architecture and patternmaking, God repeatedly instructs Moses to
speak to all who are *"chacham lev"* ("wise-hearted") emphasizing
that they are the ones to create these holy objects.[19]

     This phrase "wise-hearted" appears ten times in the
Torah, and each instance is connected to the artistic creation
of sacred structures and tools. Does "wise-hearted" refer to
some specific group of people who were invited to participate
in this creative project? Or is it that any of us, when gener-
ously sharing our creative gifts, can be understood as offering
the wisdom of our heart? In the construction of the *mishkan*,
it seems to be the latter. The text reads, "Moses called to
Betzalel and to Oholiav, and to every wise-hearted (*chacham lev*)
person whom God had endowed with wisdom in their heart
(*chacham belibo*), everyone whose heart moved them (*naso libo*) to

19 Exodus 35:10.

approach the task—to do it."[20] In standard translations, these phrases that use the Hebrew word "*lev*" ("heart") are replaced by the word "skilled," as in, "every *skilled* person whom God had endowed with *skill*." However, this misses the repetition of the word "*lev*" and the way it emphasizes the power of creating from our hearts. When we drop down into our hearts, there is wisdom to be found and there are gifts to be offered. When we create from this place, we are a part of the collective project of constructing a space for the Divine to dwell in our midst.

We read in Torah that at the center of the *mishkan* was an ever-present fire burning on the altar: "*Aish tamid tukad al hamizbe'ach, lo tikhbeh*"—"a fire [that] shall always be kept burning on the altar, never to go out."[21] Here, on behalf of the people, the priests would offer gratitude for the gifts they received, atone for their missteps, and pray for divine guidance and abundance. These entreaties and praise took the form of oil, water, and wine libations to be poured on the altar, and animal sacrifices and offerings of grain to be burnt on the altar as an offering to God. The fire on the altar of the *mishkan* offers us a powerful framework for thinking about the creative process—specifically, about how we can kindle the flame of our creativity, and fan the sparks when we need to feed that inner fire. In the spirit of multiplicity that pervades Torah study, it also offers a beautiful, fiery counterpart to the watery metaphor of the spring used by Rabbi Yochanan and Rabbi Eliezer.

Once started, a fire needs only substance and space—material and oxygen to consume. At the time of the *mishkan,* it was the task of the priests to maintain this holy fire, feeding it fresh wood and ceremoniously removing the accumulated ashes each day, in perpetuity, so the fire could breathe. We might imagine this sacred fire, requiring both material and space, as creativity. Those who cultivate it through daily attendance and practice do so not only in service of themselves;

rather, keeping this nexus point between the divine and human realms open was for the benefit of the whole community.

In our day, when the *mishkan* no longer stands, what is the sacred place where we encounter God? Perhaps we can imagine this place of all possibility residing within each of us, and that the act of tending this inner fire is now all of ours. The eternal flame is a symbol for our creativity—the passion, purpose, and inspiration that is the connection point between us and the Divine, always burning, never to go out. Like the priests, who cultivated the eternal fire of their connection and devotion through daily practice, we are wise to create a few regular habits to keep this internal fire alive. Towards this end, the creative process is both a form of release, offering us a way to clear out what has accumulated (psychically, spiritually), and a practice of cultivation, offering us a way to touch and to tend to our own inner radiance. Born from this burning, both the product and the process of creativity become our offering.

The text itself supports the reading of the *mishkan* as an internal metaphor. In another place in the text, God commands the priests: *"Ve'aish hamizbe'ach tukad bo"*—"the fire of the altar is to be kept burning on it."[22] Yet here, the Hebrew is ambiguous. *"Tukad bo"* can mean "kept burning *on it*" or "kept burning *within it/him*." From this ambiguity, we can say that the fire is both external (the one we light on the altar) and internal (the spiritual flame within ourselves). The external work we do in the world impacts and mirrors the work we do within ourselves. There is a powerful feedback loop between our hands and our heart. Our creative process externalizes something that exists within us. Thoughts and feelings become manifest through the process, allowing us to better see, understand, and potentially even transform this aspect of ourselves, thereby allowing us to become more present and available to one another, and to the Divine. In giving the Israelites instructions for creating the Temple in Jerusalem, God says *"v'asu li mikdash,*

22 Leviticus 6:2.

veshachanti bitocham"—"let them build for Me a holy sanctuary, and I will dwell among them."[23] Like *tukad bo*, *"bitocham"* can mean both "among them" and "within you all." Here, too, we can understand God as saying, "Build for me a *mikdash* (holy sanctuary), and I will dwell not only within *it*, but within each of YOU!" By creating a space for the sacred in the world, we create the real holy place for the sacred within ourselves.

The place of all possibility

Both the studio and the *beit midrash* serve the same function as the *mishkan*. Each of these are places where we come to connect with the Divine, while also struggling with meaning in our lives, the world, and our shared traditions, together with others, in community. And, crucially, they are also places where collaboration, authenticity, and creativity are welcomed— expansive spaces that are, ideally, opened up to all who would enter and participate wholeheartedly.

This has been my vision and what I have attempted to facilitate in my work over the years: to help identify, construct, and open up places that hold both the ancestral wisdom of the *beit midrash* along with the creative potential of the studio in a vibrant, alive, present-day *mishkan*. It is this desire that led me to combine all the riches I'd been gifted, interweaving the process-oriented creative practice I had grown up with— the decades of work and wisdom I inherited from my mother— with the traditional practice of textual study I inherited from my rabbinic ancestors. It's from this experimentation that JSP, as an organization devoted to cultivating creativity through Jewish wisdom, was born. What began as a portable art studio, in the spirit of the original *mishkan* (my spouse and I carting around boxes of supplies and sacred texts in the trunk of our car to bring to sometimes skeptical participants) has grown

---

23 Exodus 25:8.

into a national organization dedicated to bringing creativity
back to the center of our lives. Through community programs,
immersive experiences, creative facilitator training, and professional development partnerships, JSP is working to activate the
creative power of the Jewish community and beyond. We partner
with organizations that are feeling stuck, or are looking to
make big changes, to help them reconnect to the power of their
imagination to envision new possibilities. We work with
schools where educators are feeling burnt out to help them reconnect to the creative power within to sustain them through
the challenges of teaching. We support groups of clergy that are
seeking ways to reconnect with the Divine—that source
of energy and inspiration that first called them to the path of
spiritual leadership. And we are building and supporting a
far-reaching international network of facilitators to extend
this work into communities across the globe.

    At the core of our work is the creative practice I've
mentioned throughout this book: the Jewish Studio Process.
Part textual learning, part spiritual practice, part art-making
method, the Jewish Studio Process is a practice that allows
each of us (regardless of cultural background or artistic training)
to add our own voice to the ongoing chain of interpretation
and to engage in a meaningful process of self-discovery through
imagination, intuition, and a spirit of play. Using the creative
process as a form of inquiry into sacred text brings together the
art studio and the *beit midrash* to create something new: an experiential form of learning that reveals new dimensions of sacred
text while also pointing towards how the text speaks to each
of our personal lives. The result is a new understanding of self,
a renewed relationship to the Divine, fresh interpretations of
ancient text, creations that never before existed, and a sense
of connection—to ancient Jewish wisdom, to those in our
community, and to our own deepest selves.

    Torah is renewed by our creative engagement, as are we.
When we bring the fullness of who we are to this age-old
interpretive practice, we make space for new stories, insights,

ideas, and questions. As God conveys to Moses all of the
materials and measurements required to construct the Temple,
God says: "Build this for Me, and I will dwell within you."[24]
The work we do with our hands and our imaginations—the way
that we process and engage the world—clears out and creates
that space for the Divine to dwell within our heart and opens the
way to the place of all possibility.

---

24 Exodus 25:8.

The Jewish Studio Process

The Torah of Creativity provides the conceptual framework that fuels the Jewish Studio Process. In the first two chapters, we explored the dynamic ecosystem of Torah and creativity. In this chapter, I lay out the framework and methodology that ground the Jewish Studio Process, giving you the basic steps to start to explore on your own.

The Jewish Studio Process is a way of engaging with Torah beyond, through, and alongside the interpretations that have already been written—by traditional commentators, by pop culture, by our parents and teachers. Through the Process, we are invited to bring our authentic questions, needs, and struggles to the page and open to what emerges. The Process approaches Torah with the belief that the text welcomes all of us and all of who we are, granting us the freedom to read Torah in ways that are true to the text, and true to ourselves, even if what emerges is perhaps quite different from interpretations we've heard in the past. Each one of us brings new perspectives that can offer new insights. In this way, the encounter between us and the text is always unique: this exact moment in our personal lives, and in our collective history, has never come before and will never come again. When we engage Torah in this way, words and phrases take on new meanings, and the text is able to stay alive and dynamic, even as the words themselves remain the same. Tradition stays relevant by yielding ever-new insights as our needs and perspectives evolve.

When we approach Torah through the Jewish Studio Process, we stir the cauldron of possibilities in which the alchemy between ourselves and the wisdom of these ancient texts can be born. This process of inquiry and art-making can be intense, but it can be (and often is) delightful as well— in the sensory pleasure of engaging with color, shape, sounds, movement, or language; the revitalizing energy of creative expression; and the clarity of new insight. While this may seem radically experimental and improvisational, it's actually deeply rooted in Jewish mystical thought and traditional study practices.

The Zohar gives the following evocative description of the pleasure of creative process with Torah:

> *Rabbi Shimon opened his discourse with a line from Isaiah upon which he would expound. He quoted: I have put My words in your mouth (Isaiah 51:16). He interprets: It is vital for a person to engage in Torah, for with every word of Torah that is innovated in the mouths of humans, a new heaven is created. It was taught: In the hour that a word of Torah is innovated in the mouth of a human being, that word rises up and presents itself before God, and the Holy Blessed One lifts that word and kisses it and crowns it with seventy crowns, engraved and inscribed ... The Holy One, the Ancient of Days, breathes in that word and it pleases God more than anything ... On this it is written in Isaiah: As the new heavens and the new earth that I make endure before Me (Isaiah 66:22). Notice that it is not written "I made" in the past tense, but rather "I make," in the present. The world is continually made and remade through innovative words of Torah.*[1]

This passage offers us an intoxicating image of the sheer delight that is available in the process of spiritual creativity and interpretive innovation. As this passage describes, we can imagine the words themselves reveling in the freedom

---

1   Zohar, Hakdama Sefer haZohar 1:4b–5a.

to expand into multiple, new dimensions. Here, the Zohar offers us a view of the process of creative interpretation as intimate, embodied, and deeply pleasurable: God kisses, crowns, and inhales these new words of Torah, delighting in each new iteration of meaning. The improvisational interpretive process described here is one that is both playful and serious; in which ideas are both deeply held and joyfully allowed to evolve. These threads of creativity, as both a form of profound sacred play and a mode of engagement with Torah interwoven with our own creativity, have always been present in Jewish tradition. When we bring our voice to Torah in this way, we not only discover interpretations that speak to our own personal lives, but, like the authors of the Zohar, we can imagine that we are bringing about delight and joy on a cosmic level, which reverberates throughout the world.

The traditional study of Talmud gives us another framework for this form of creativity, in both the text itself and the way it is learned. The layout of a page of Talmud is a graphic representation of the process-oriented polyvocality that characterizes traditional Jewish study. In the center of the page is a short text from the Mishnah (one of the earliest rabbinic commentaries on the Torah), followed by the Gemara (the earliest layer of commentary on the Mishnah, written in late antiquity); and then framing this central text are columns of later commentaries by generations of medieval scholars (Rashi, a singularly influential Torah scholar from the eleventh century, and the authors of Tosefot, a collection of commentaries from the following generations). Taken all together, this *Tetris*-like textual architecture comprises a multilayered, multigenerational discussion on what the Torah (broadly defined) is trying to teach us. The fact that the many voices represented on a page of Talmud don't always agree is a feature—not a bug—of this system. Underlying this polyvocality, and the back-and-forth cross-pollination of ideas, is an ethos of perpetual probing and intergenerational dialogue that is inscribed in the Talmudic page design itself.

But it is not only in the material on the page; it is also in the way that traditional Jewish study occurs: in dynamic exchange with a teacher, the text, and a *chavruta*, or study partner. As mentioned earlier, a *chavruta* is a peer with whom one engages in a collaborative dialogue about the text—arguing, puzzling through, and improvising ideas with each other. And the *beit midrash* is not meant to be a quiet or secluded place; rather, it is a place of discussion and passionate debate— and even occasional singing. Numerous conversations happen at once, on a host of different topics. Learners move at their own pace and follow where their conversation takes them. This exploratory, expressive way of learning entertains multiple meanings and interpretations, holds a space for many different learning styles, and encourages learners to come up with better questions, rather than only seeking one right answer. The word "*chavruta*" is related to the word for friend or peer, "*chaver*," and to the verb "*chibur*," to bind together. Collaborative, creative engagement with sacred text binds us to each other, to the generations that have come before, to our own innate creativity, and to the Divine. This act of textual engagement creates a rich, multivocal tapestry of interpretation and, in so doing, stitches each learner into the fabric of tradition. In contrast to the "sage on the stage" paradigm— the lone genius or wise man (it is usually a man) in the spotlight while everyone else is left in the dark—*chavruta* learning shines the light around the room and explores what is revealed in both the bright spots and shadows, together. Learning arises communally, as a mutual process of growth and discovery that acknowledges the layers of collective history and personal experience.

Life itself is built on interconnection; our very bodies are constituted by millions of microorganisms. The biological world, in which we are completely enmeshed, is a process of continual cocreation and interdependence—a reality our social and communal lives reflect as well. When we come together in *chavruta*, we are subtly and powerfully reminding ourselves of the ultimate reality of our interconnection. As we bind ourselves to each other through *chavruta* study, we learn the ins and outs of deep listening, caring connection, and appreciation for the uniqueness of the other.[2] We learn how to be in relationship. This seemingly modest practice of *chavruta* grows in us the skills necessary to build a larger culture of care. What could be more important today?

By honoring the diversity of the human experience and the uniqueness of each person, we arrive at the most complete, and therefore most profound, truths. A midrash on the revelation at Mount Sinai illustrates the value of such multiple perspectives. The story tells of the moment when the Torah was revealed:

> *God appeared like a picture, visible from all angles, a thousand people may gaze on it and it gazes on all of them. So is the Holy One, blessed be God. When the Divine spoke [at Sinai] every individual person maintained: To me the word spoke! It is not written "I am the Lord your [singular] God," rather "I am the Lord your [plural] God," I am the Source that flows through and connects everyone and everything. Said R. Yose: "In accordance with each and everyone's personal capacities did the word speak to them."*[3]

The Torah each of us is able to receive is shaped by our unique perspectives and experiences, but none of us receive it alone. At Sinai, God spoke "face-to-face" with each of us, in the presence of all of us. We each bring a fragment of the whole picture, which can only be deciphered when these fragments are brought together. To return Torah to the place of all possibility, we need each other. It is only together that we can meaningfully bring the fullness and complexity of ancient Jewish wisdom deep

---

2 For a deep dive into the qualities cultivated in *chavruta* study, see Elie Holzer and Orit Kent, *A Philosophy of Havruta: Understanding and Teaching the Art of Text Study in Pairs* (Boston: Academic Studies Press, 2013).

3 Yalkut Shimoni, Yitro 286.

into our own hearts and out into the world. Our perspectives, opinions, and creative additions weave together and coexist alongside one another, echoing the multilayered voices on the page and the many *chavruta* pairs learning together in the *beit midrash*.

From study to studio

The creative approach to Torah study that is the foundation of the Jewish Studio Process builds on these principles of multiplicity and collaboration, as well as the deeper understanding of Torah as a source of vitality and creativity. It is a methodology that combines a practice of art-making developed by my mother and mentor Pat B. Allen (called the Open Studio Process) with what I call the Torah of Creativity. The Jewish Studio Process moves from the *beit midrash* to the art studio; from a black-and-white page packed with words to a blank sheet waiting to be filled with lines, shape, and color. This practice provides each of us with a simple but profound method not only to find ourselves in the Torah and the Torah in ourselves, but also to encode within us the skills and capacities to imagine and bring forth new possibilities for ourselves and our world. Exploring the world through this creative process is a practice for learning how to make space within us for those wild, vital parts of ourselves that often get silenced or shunted to the side. In this practice of art-making, the river of creativity can freely flow through us as we encounter forgotten or unknown parts of ourselves. And eventually (like Rabbi Eliezer in the last chapter), we might offer to the world some of what we find: our own unique light, wisdom, and beauty.

Across time, a core aspect of Judaism has been its iterative capacity: its invitation to return over and over to the same materials but with new questions and understandings, lending our texts a limitless ability to shift and change as circumstances demand. This is, in part, what has allowed the textual tradition to be a force of survival and renewal as well as a resource for envisioning the world as it could be. The Jewish Studio Process is in this lineage of spiritual innovation and practical preservation, allowing and empowering us to meet the challenges of the world we live in.

In my time developing this methodology, I have found that it is infinitely adaptable. While I have most often engaged in visual art and embodied movement, I have seen this practice work powerfully within any material or medium. Further, the Process can be meaningfully engaged solo or in a group. Although, as explained earlier in this chapter, the Process draws on *chavruta* learning, it can still be generative when done on one's own, as a personal creative spiritual practice. Rather than engaging with multiple voices other than your own, if you're doing the Process alone, I recommend tuning into the multiplicity of voices that exist within you, and giving each space to be heard.

The Process progresses in four basic stages: inquiry, intention, exploration, and reflection. The following explanation of these four stages is a distilled introduction to the Jewish Studio Process. You can use this as a reference guide for when you are inspired to try this practice at home.

Stage 1: Inquiry

A rabbinic commentary on the creation story found in the Torah says, "The Holy One gazed into the Torah and created the world."[4] In this interpretation, the Torah itself contains the blueprints for the world. In beginning to create the world, God looks at the Torah for instructions and guidance. If we take this idea beyond God and Torah, we might say that this midrash teaches that when a creator (any creator) begins to create, learning Torah can ignite, inspire, and guide their creative process. It is for this reason that we begin the Jewish Studio Process with reading, and discussing, a bit of Jewish text. Torah study helps

4   Beresheit Rabbah 1:1.

us generate new ideas, push at the limits of our own consciousness and internal perceptions, and tap into an energetic stream
that has been flowing for generations.

Begin with a text that intrigues you. This could be from
the Torah, Prophets, Psalms, Talmud, Zohar, or any sacred text
from the Jewish literary canon. Start by reading through the
text out loud. Maybe read it a few times. Hearing the words
on the page spoken out loud can change how the words resonate
within you, and open up new possibilities for interpretation.
Take your time. As you listen, make note of anything that
strikes you about the text. Include anything that sparks your
curiosity or captures your interest, even (especially) if you don't
quite know why. Ask yourself what you already know (or think
you know) about this text. Hold each of these "known" things
lightly and consider them from different angles. Notice what
else comes into your awareness: Does it call to mind past
teachings you've learned? Does it touch on something in your
life today? Does it speak to something you are reading or
studying in another area of your life? Does it evoke something
happening in the world at this moment? As you hear the
words of the text spoken aloud, notice where the material is
hitting you on a personal level, such as memories, dreams,
experiences, desires, fears, or joys that it brings up in your own
life. What might these ideas, thoughts, feelings, or memories
offer your understanding of this text?

In the inquiry stage of the process, all thoughts and
feelings are welcome in the room. We bring our unique life
experiences and perspectives to the text, unearthing new
understandings, images, and questions, while we allow the
words on the page to reveal thoughts or feelings in ourselves
that we may not yet be consciously aware of.

Torah can comfort, agitate, confuse, or inspire us. In fact,
a single text has the ability to do all of this at once. A particular
text may ring hollow one day, and inspire us the next. In the
inquiry stage of this process, we permit ourselves to feel whatever comes up in response to what's on the page with openness

and kindness towards ourselves, whomever we may be studying with, and towards the text itself. For instance, the Jacob
and Esau story may spark memories, associations, and feelings about our own sibling rivalries, the role of birth order
in our relationship with our parents, or what it means to heal
the cycle of generational trauma. We may not be thinking consciously about these family dynamics, but sometimes reading
a story—whether for the first or the fiftieth time—can bring
up feelings and insights that weren't obvious to us before.
The text acts as a mirror, reflecting back to us who we are in
that moment, who we have been, and who we might become.

Here are five **guidelines for inquiry** to help you get
started in this stage of the Jewish Studio Process:

Bring who you are in this moment to the text. To engage
in this practice, you do not need to be well-versed in Torah.
You do not need to "believe" in God. You do not need to think
of yourself as "religious" or "spiritual." You don't have to
be in a good mood or act (or feel) reverent towards the text.
No part of yourself needs to be silenced or shunted to the
side. Whether you are feeling grief, anxiety, rage, sadness,
or confusion—all of those feelings are valid and true in that
moment. The text is there for us no matter what state we are in.

It's okay to read the text out of context. Words and
phrases contain potency and meaning beyond the particular
passage where we first find them. Sometimes the broader
context of the narrative is helpful and provides its own meaning.
But in this stage, it can be liberating to spend time with a
passage that speaks to you without knowing (or while intention-
ally forgetting!) the entire backstory. Reading out of context
can free us to allow new and unexpected meanings to emerge.

Hold previous interpretations lightly. Sometimes new
interpretations build off older ones. But other times, we need
to release old interpretations to make space for new perspectives.
Making space for new understandings is a valid way of honoring the text and staying true to the interpretative process.
These new interpretations don't replace old ones; rather,

they exist side by side. All interpretations, new and old, are available for us to connect to when we most need them.

Feel into the text with your whole self. Torah study can be informed by all parts of us: our somatic experience, our intellect, our intuition and emotions. Allow yourself the space to tune into your embodied awareness. How does this text make you feel in your body? What feelings are coming up? Does your heart beat a little faster? Does your stomach drop with dread? Do your eyes water as you imagine what one of the characters is going through? Deeper insights can arise when we invite the fullness of who we are to the experience.

Follow interpretations that bring you greater vitality and possibility. The Jewish tradition teaches that there are seventy faces of Torah—that is, seventy (or more!) ways of interpreting every word. A single passage can be understood in countless, and often contradictory, ways. Which of these feel hopeful and helpful? Which make you feel supported, inspired, or challenged in a fruitful way on this particular day? You are entitled to put your energy towards those! No matter what you find, know that there is something new and generative for you in the text. When we approach text with an open mind, we find there is always something for us, just waiting to be discovered.

Stage 2: Intention

At the end of the inquiry stage of the Jewish Studio Process, you might feel animated or excited by something that came up. The invitation now is to look for the spark of curiosity, inspiration, or strong emotion that is calling you to be explored more fully and use this as a springboard to create an intention. This second stage of intention-setting functions as a bridge from the inquiry stage to the exploration stage that follows.

Setting an intention serves multiple purposes. First, it is a way to notice where you're at in the present moment, which may be very different from how you were feeling when you began. Intention-setting is also how you create boundaries for

yourself and focus your experience. Many thoughts and feelings likely came up during the inquiry stage; you have every
right to explore any of these feelings during art-making—
or not to! You are in charge of how you want to use this time
and what to focus on. By setting an intention, you decide
what to invite into your creative process, and what to leave aside.

Take a few deep breaths to ground yourself as you transition from inquiry into the intention-setting stage. As you do,
allow what feels most alive to you to bubble to the surface.
Often, an intention arises from something that snags your
attention—that place where you feel a little unsettled, cloudy,
or intrigued. This may be a word, phrase, or question, or something about the process of engaging with the text. Perhaps you
want to delve into the specific meaning of the language, or
perhaps you're at the end of a long day and you're just looking
for some tranquility. Your intention might also include how
you want to feel during the next stage of exploration through
art-making (like joyous or free), or what you want to leave
behind (like worry or stress). Your intention is used to focus
and direct your process. It's possible that your intention may
be crystal clear, or perhaps it feels muddied and unsure.
In this case, make an intention to find your intention through
the creative process!

An intention is a practical tool for opening up connection to the realm of serendipity and spirit. In this practice
intention is made as a simple statement of what we wish to
receive in the creative process. Intentions are worded posi-
tively, in the present tense, without using striving language
like "want" or "try." On a spiritual level, intention is how we
invite something that is both beyond and deep within us into
our creative process. Intention is a key that opens a channel
between you and this force, whatever you choose to call it
(or even if you don't call it anything). In this way, your creative
process becomes a form of self-divination, and your intention
is like a prayer that has already been answered. Once you have
your intention, write it down; you'll revisit it later in the process.

Tips for formulating your intention
If you're not sure how to start, you might experiment with one of these phrases and then fill in the rest of the sentence:

> *Through my creative process, I explore…*
> *Through my creative process, I experience…*
> *Through my creative process, I open to…*
> *Through my creative process, I release…*

Here are some sample intentions, to give you an idea what others have written during the Jewish Studio Process sessions we've done in the past:

> *I discover what else this text has to teach me.*
> *I explore the interplay between light and dark in the text.*
> *I open to gratitude.*
> *I experience a sense of calmness.*
> *I release anxiety and fear and open to the joy of creating.*

Your intention is a way of actively partnering with the Divine; paradoxically, it is also an act of surrender. Once you've set your intention, you no longer need to actively focus on it. You can let go into the flow of the creative process and "make art about it!" To assist yourself in this step, I recommend a practice I call "set it and forget it": after you've written your intention down, flip over that piece of paper or turn the page in your journal. This physical gesture communicates to your conscious and unconscious mind that there is no need to focus on, or even remember, what you wrote down. This is a practice in learning to surrender and release, a gesture of trust in yourself and the power you have to direct your life. It is a wonderful microcosm of the creative process itself.

Stage 3: Exploration

This stage of the process allows us to explore unknown aspects of the text and to bring these into relationship with unknown aspects of ourselves. In this practice, our art-making—whether on the canvas, the dance floor, or the notepad—is not dictated by a preconceived idea of what "art" should look or sound like. It is an exercise in open exploration. This stage of the process is about letting the thinking mind relax and making space for other parts of ourselves to find expression, like our intuition, imagination, emotion, and memory. Improvisational, process-oriented art-making gives us something pleasurable to do and focus on (much like the flow state described in the last chapter), allowing our nervous system to relax so other parts of ourselves have the space to emerge. It's often helpful to set a timer in advance so that you stop at a preset time, rather than worrying about how long you have left while you're in the exploration stage.

Any modality can be used: movement, writing, music, painting, sculpting—you name it. You can use the highest quality materials from the art supply store, or your child's crayons, or some leaves and sticks that you found in the backyard. You can use a modality that is familiar to you, or one that is new. At some point, either way, I encourage you to step outside your comfort zone and try a modality you've never used before. If you're a painter, try moving your body; if you're a writer, try picking up a set of watercolors. And if you don't have experience using art materials, the simple act of picking up some colored pens and flowing from there can be a very generative venture outside your comfort zone. Working with an unfamiliar modality can be liberating since we approach the materials unencumbered by past training or experience, and can hopefully release unhelpful expectations about what "good" looks or sounds like. This "beginner's mind" (as some Zen Buddhists call it) can allow us to move more easily into a place of experimentation, curiosity, and delight.

Once you've selected a modality for the exploration stage of the process, begin by finding a material that sparks your interest and simply start by making marks on the page. If you are working with your body, you might start with one small, simple gesture. If you are writing, you might start with a few minutes of freewriting. If you are sculpting, you might start just by moving the material in your hands in a way that feels pleasing, noticing the different shapes that form. Whatever it is, make small gestures, without any particular rhyme or reason, just allowing and noticing what shows up.

It's essential to follow what feels good, whatever is energizing for you in a given moment. If you're painting, that may mean covering the page with a color that looks particularly beautiful to you today, noticing the gradations of light and dark as you move your brush. Or, if you're working with your body, maybe circling your wrists as you find a stretch that you didn't realize you needed. Do this until the next thing sparks your interest—the bright allure of yellow, or a desire to move another part of your body—and then follow that. By simply following pleasure, suddenly your page has turned from entirely turquoise to having big droplets of yellow, which then calls for orange squiggles, which begin to look like birds, so you add on beaks and wings—even though you've never seen a bird that looks like this and you had no plan to paint fantastical birds when you began.

To follow pleasure is to notice these impulses and to let them lead you into the place of all possibility. Both the sensual call of the materials and the simple structure of the process open new pathways that go beyond the conscious mind. Your piece does not need to "make sense." Rather, it should feel *alive*. You may have sat down to paint thinking about sadness and found yourself painting warmth and light. Follow that. Don't censor yourself if what you are doing doesn't follow any logic or conform to preconceived ideas about "art" or "expression." The goal of this step is to relax the thinking mind and begin to activate different capacities. Soft, open, engaged—it is from this place that intuition and imagination begin to speak and we allow ourselves to act as a vessel, receiving the flow of what wants to come through.

Rules of the studio
Because this is such an open-ended, process-oriented practice, we've found that a core set of studio rules provides the necessary spiritual guardrails and creative constraints to allow us to surrender, but not become ungrounded. Together, the studio rules and steps of the Jewish Studio Process offer a ritualized container for us to safely enter, dwell within, and depart from refreshed and renewed. Whether you are moving your body, playing an instrument, or taking a paint brush to a canvas, there are four rules to help guide and support your art-making: **follow pleasure**; **no comment**; **notice everything**; and **keep going**.

1   Follow pleasure
Following pleasure is the primary guideline to follow during art-making. When you are in a state of pleasure and relaxation, you become open to new ideas coming to and through you.

2   No comment
Avoid commenting on your own or on anyone else's piece— even (and especially) to say how much you like it. This is particularly important when practicing with others. Comments will naturally arise within you. As they do, invite them into your own process (rather than sharing them with others) and see what they have to offer you. Why did that comment arise and what might it mean for you?

3   Notice everything
Everything that arises during the art-making stage is part of the process; the process can hold it all. Allow yourself to notice what comes up during this stage of the practice and see if it sparks any further curiosity worth following. Even if it's small

annoyances, like your to-do list nagging at the edge of
your mind, or ambient noise like traffic or birds outside the
window; everything is potential fodder for the process.
The same is true for feelings, whether stress, annoyance,
sadness, elation, or anything else that arises.

4   Keep going

Stay with the process for the full amount of time. We often
want to stop when something "looks nice," thinking that we
don't want to "mess it up," but if we stay with it, this is often
the moment right before the next breakthrough. "Keep going"
can mean continuing to add to your piece, or it can mean not
adding anything at all, but continuing to stay in relationship
to what's there, exploring it from different angles, and feeling
what comes up for you.

Stage 4: Reflection

The final stage of the Jewish Studio Process is reflection,
in which we witness our practice through freewriting and,
if it feels right, we read what we wrote aloud. We call this
witness-writing and witness-reading; in it, our stillness
makes space for insights to arise through what we've created
and the process itself. Here we interact with our piece in a
similar way to how we interacted with Torah during the
inquiry stage: curious about what it has to say, letting it speak
to and through us.

To transition to the first piece of the reflection, witness-
writing, come to a comfortable (or uncomfortable!) stopping
place in your art-making. Take a few long, slow, deep breaths.
Then, start by noticing what you see and feel. Take a few sentences to write it down in descriptive detail, without coming
to any conclusions about what, exactly, it is. For example, if
you have been painting, rather than naming your image and
attaching a story to it right away ("I see myself at age five in
my grandmother's house"), start by describing the color and
shape of the figure on the page: "I see a small figure in yellow

next to a large rectangle." The mind immediately wants to make sense out of what we've created. Often, these stories are the familiar ones that we are used to telling ourselves about our life; instead, we want to make space for the process to offer new insights, stories, and visions. Describing your creation plainly at first, in terms of shape and sensation, allows you to slow down, and to keep the thinking mind at bay for a while longer. After that you can begin to allow stories to emerge.

As you write, notice how you feel. Be sure to include everything, even extraneous details. Try not to censor yourself. "I need to use the bathroom" or "I'm feeling bored with this" are as noteworthy as thoughts that seem profound or poetic. Just as you allowed yourself to be moved by something beyond your rational mind while you were making art, now allow your pen to be moved without thinking about what it is you're writing. Continue freewriting for about ten minutes. Towards the end of your witness-writing, revisit your intention. What, if anything, does this piece, or your experience of making it, have to say to your intention? In what ways might it speak to the text you learned? Write this down as a final reflection.

Witness-writing guide
- ↝ Observe your creation in the most basic way possible: describe shapes, colors, movement. Refrain from naming or explaining characters or objects.
- ↝ Jot down what you are feeling as you observe your piece and let the effects of engaging with the material settle into you.
- ↝ Follow any stories that begin to develop.
- ↝ Consider dialoguing with your image, or a particular piece of your image.
- ↝ You may ask your piece what, if anything, it has to say to the text you learned at the start of your process.
- ↝ Ask your piece in what ways, if any, it speaks to the intention that you set at the beginning of the process.

↝   Allow everything that arises into your consciousness to
       come out onto the page.
↝   Follow what sparks your attention and see where
       it takes you.

The last piece of reflection is witness-reading. This is the
practice of reading some or all of what you've written out loud;
it is always an invitation, not a requirement. Whether you
are practicing in a group or solo, the point of witness-reading
is to hear your own words as they have come to you and
through you. Reading aloud to oneself can be clarifying and
empowering. Something happens when you speak your
own words aloud: they vibrate with energy and spirit, and you
hear them differently than when you're reading them silently
on the page. To read aloud in this way allows for new levels of
meaning and resonance to become apparent.

        If you are practicing in a group setting, when reading
what you've written, don't provide context, commentary,
casual asides, or framing. Simply read the words on your page,
whether they are complete sentences, stream of consciousness,
or gibberish. This reading is done as a formal practice. If you've
created visual art, you can hold it up for others to see. Once
someone has finished reading, the group thanks them, to
acknowledge their offering, and the space is opened up for
the next person who wants to read. There is no discussion
or commenting. In this way, this space is held as a sacred
ceremony with clear ritual guidelines and flow. I recommend
choosing some action to mark the end of this formal process,
be it simply a deep, meditative breath, blowing out a candle
you may have lit at the start of the process, or stretching your
body—something that creates a temporal boundary around
the process and allows you to honor yourself and the experience
you made time for.

Common roadblocks

In my time teaching the Jewish Studio Process, I've noticed some common obstacles that people run into that can hamper their ability to experience the full potential of this method. Perhaps the most common, which I have heard over and over again from participants in my workshops, are doubts about one's innate creativity, or the value of this kind of exploratory art-making. "But I'm really not creative!" "How could drawing pictures actually help me in my life?" Rather than trying to shut down these anxieties, if these thoughts arise, make space for them. Though it may sound counterintuitive, even seemingly negative emotions have something to teach us. What anxieties or desires are they speaking to? What are they trying to protect? It is natural to feel apprehension when exploring new experiences or perspectives. Honor these doubts and invite them along for the ride.

Another obstacle is feeling rushed due to lack of time, and the difficulty of simply quieting the general stress of life in order to focus on the present moment. These feelings can be quite distracting when you're trying to move your consciousness into a contemplative and meditative mode. Notice what arises when you feel rushed or stressed, particularly around your relationship to time, and recognize that this subjective feeling of time can change. The same amount of time you give to the creative process might feel spacious one week and sparse the next. Know that just coming to the page and engaging in the process is a huge step. Let yourself feel good about setting aside whatever time you have.

Lastly, related to those same doubts about artistic abilities, you may experience a fear of "messing up." This can hold you back from fully exploring your feelings, intuitions, and creative potential. There's no such thing as messing up in this process—in fact, messy is good! When things feel overly precious, you might feel pressure to use your materials well. Sometimes, the less it feels like "art," the freer we become. If you're feeling stuck in this way, try this: start with a

piece of paper that isn't pristine, like a piece of scrap paper,
or a paper bag, and use the most basic materials, like a ballpoint pen, or a highlighter. In this approach, we have a slightly
different equation of "product" and "process," beyond the
binary that is usually put forth. The process is eminently important as it allows us to have a full creative experience, while the
"product" becomes our memento of the journey we've been on.
Not only that, what we've created is a repository of the energy,
insights, and struggle of our process that we can return to
for future inspiration and sustenance. In this way, both product
and process are intimately connected aspects of a holistic experience that give us access to a sense of wholeness and wisdom
within ourselves.

Here's a recap of the Jewish Studio Process as a reference guide for when you try this at home:

1   Inquiry
↝   Start by picking a text. Read it alone or study it
        in *chavruta*.
↝   Notice what comes up—excitement, agitation,
        confusion, and so on.

2   Intention
↝   Write down an intention for the art-making process.

3   Exploration
↝   Make art in an improvisational manner, letting yourself
        be led by pleasure and whatever sparks your energy and
        interest in the moment.

4   Reflection
↝   Write down your observations, responses, and feelings
        that arise from what you've created and the experience
        of creating it.
↝   Check back in with your intention and ask how your
        exploration reflects or expands on it, and how it might
        have transformed in the process.

Coda

Grounded in and emerging from the conceptual framework of the Torah of Creativity, the Jewish Studio Process offers a way for each one of us to find new meaning and insight from ancient Jewish wisdom. Through the unique alchemy of who we are, the passage of sacred text we are looking at, and the moment in time in which we are living, something new is able to be born. The knowledge and insight that emerges can not only support us personally in the questions, struggles, and longings of our lives, but are added to the ongoing evolution of collective meaning for others to draw on as well.

How does all this sound? If it feels like a lot, take your time. If you are excited and ready to get started, jump in. May you find the pleasure in this process and may it nourish your mind, body, soul, and spirit. And thank you in advance for all you will give to the swirl of collective meaning that is the birthright of each and everyone of us.

The next section will introduce five core principles that guide the Jewish Studio Process, each carving out its own pathway to the place of all possibility.

PATHS THROUGH
THE PLACE OF ALL POSSIBILITY

Setting Out on the Path

Having explored the intersections of Torah and creativity, and introduced the Jewish Studio Process (a methodology that combines the two), we now turn to five pathways you can travel in your creative process, in your explorations of Torah, and in navigating the struggles, joys, and questions of your own life. Each pathway consists of a fragment of Jewish text that yields insight into the innate creativity at the core of our humanity. Some are drawn from ethical teachings, some come from stories centering on God's attributes and actions, and some are from stories focusing on key biblical figures. In our examination of these texts, each character (including God) can be seen as an embodiment of qualities and capacities that exist within each of us, and the situations they encounter as having symbolic corollaries in our own lives.

These texts offer us guidance for how to work with the stuff of our lives and the world, and support us in cultivating our creativity as we move through the challenges and changes that life brings. These paths are here to support you in your journey through the place of all possibility, but ultimately it's not about these specific paths themselves. Rather, these chapters offer a model of how to work with Torah to discover, create, and traverse all paths that call out for you to explore. Take what's here and add to it. Your journey is your own, and we're all in this together.

בצלם אלהים

BeTzelem Elohim

WE ARE CREATED CREATIVE

תהו ובהו

Tohu vaVohu

CREATION COMES FROM CHAOS AND VOID

לך-לך

Lekh Lekha

WE ARE CALLED TO JOURNEY INTO THE UNKNOWN

אהיה אשר אהיה

Ehyeh Asher Ehyeh

GOD IS PROCESS

הפך בה

Hafokh Bah

WHAT ELSE COULD THIS BE?

ויברא אלהים את האדם בצלמו **בצלם אלהים** ברא אתו.

*Vayivra Elohim et ha'adam betzalmo, **betzelem Elohim** bara oto.*

GOD CREATED HUMANKIND IN GOD'S IMAGE;
IN THE IMAGE OF GOD DID GOD CREATE IT.
GENESIS 1:27

We Are Created Creative

In the image

God's creative power is intimately linked to our own. In the
first chapter of Genesis, we are given the beautiful, essential
teaching that human beings are created *betzelem Elohim*—
in the image of the Divine.[1] A common interpretation of this
verse is that *betzelem Elohim* means that each human life is
sacred. No matter your age, race, gender, sexual orientation,
or any other facet of identity, you are made in God's image.
Every human life is to be cherished and respected. But there is
more in this verse waiting to be uncovered. In order to understand what it may mean for us to be made in God's image, first
we must more deeply explore the nature of the Divine. There
are many stories we could turn to to get a sense of who or what
God is, and since God encompasses all, each would paint a
slightly different picture, emphasizing different qualities and
attributes. For our purposes, let's go back to the very beginning
of beginnings to explore how God is first portrayed in the
Hebrew Bible.

    The Torah opens with the words: *"Beresheit bara Elohim et
hashamayim ve'et ha'aretz."* "In the beginning, God created the
heavens and the earth."[2] Commentators across the generations
have conjectured about why Torah begins with the creation of

1   Genesis 1:27.
2   Genesis 1:1.

the world, and what meaning these verses might have to
offer us in our own lives. While it may perhaps seem obvious
that Torah should start with the beginning of creation,
the renowned eleventh-century Jewish commentator Rabbi
Shlomo Yitzchaki (commonly known by the acronym Rashi)
doesn't take this as a given. Rather, he wonders why the Torah
doesn't instead start with the commandments, the directives
for how we're meant to live in the world and relate to each
other.[3] For Rashi, Torah is primarily a book of laws and instructions for proper conduct. So, Rashi seems to be asking, why
is it important to know how we got here? Isn't it more essential to know how we ought to live, now that we're here?
Rashi answers his own question by saying that the Torah opens
with this act of creativity to assert God's ultimate power:
to conceive of God as the creator of the cosmos is to know that
God owns the world and everything in it, an idea that then
sets the tone for how we read everything that follows.

But what if starting with God's creation of the universe
is less about asserting God's power, and more about inviting us
to access and activate our own creative potential? What if it's
about coming to understand our creativity as the way we build,
shape, and imagine new realities and relationships? What if it
is about helping us to know creativity as the most generative,
dynamic, and potent aspect of being human—showing us that
all possibilities are born from our innate creative potential?
As this first verse of Genesis conveys, the God of the Torah is one
who brings the world into being. Up until this point, the only
thing we know about God is that God is creative. So, to say that
we are made *betzelem Elohim*, in the divine image, is to say that
we are fundamentally creative creations. As the great philosopher Rabbi Joseph Soloveitchik writes in his seminal work
The Lonely Man of Faith, "There is no doubt that the term 'image
of God' in the first account refers to man's inner charismatic

3   Rashi on Genesis 1:1.

endowment as a creative being."[4] The Torah begins with God's creation of the world to teach us that creativity is essential to God—and to us.

From *beresheit bara Elohim,* all else that follows—the creation of starlight and birdsong, soft grass and sweet nectar—comes from this initial act of creativity. The opening lines of Genesis continue, elaborating on the conditions of this first creative act: "The Earth was chaos and void with darkness on the surface of the deep and God's breath hovering over the water."[5] Isn't this how all creative processes begin? We start in darkness, a state of not knowing, not yet understanding or being able to see clearly. There is chaos: jumbled confusion, questions, all that doesn't yet make sense. And there is a void—an open space pulsing with energy. We start by hovering above the surface, that which is visible and known, as we gaze into the depths. And there is spirit—our own, God's, both together—that begins to shimmer with aliveness as our curiosity is ignited and engaged. All creativity begins this way.

Formed in the divine image, creativity is woven into the fabric of who we are. We are created creative. It is at the core of what it means to be human, and of how we connect to the Divine. To more deeply understand our own innate creativity and how we might draw on this power within us to shape the life and world we seek, we can look to God's creative process in shaping the heavens and the earth.

With beginner's mind

As we continue to mine God's creation of the world to glean insight for our own creative process, let us stay with this opening phrase of Torah to see what more might be uncovered in these initial words. Commonly translated as "in the

4 Joseph Dov Soloveitchik, *The Lonely Man of Faith* (New York: Doubleday, 1992), 12.
5 Genesis 1:2.

beginning," *"beresheit"* can be understood in myriad ways.
Parsing this phrase, the *"be"* at the beginning is a conjugation
that can mean "in," "with," or "by means of," while the word
"reisheit" means "first." In addition to "in the beginning," trans-
lators have interpreted this opening phrase of Torah to mean
"with the beginning," "by means of the first," or "when God
began." One of my favorite interpretations of this line is from
my friend, colleague, and teacher Rabbi Benay Lappe, which
she shared when we were once studying this verse together:
"With the first way of seeing or perceiving things, God created."
Another way of saying this is: "With beginner's mind, God
created the world."

"Beginner's mind" (known as "s*hoshin*," in Japanese) is a
concept from Zen Buddhism that describes a certain openness
and lack of preconceptions. In his book *Zen Mind, Beginner's Mind*,
Zen teacher Shunryū Suzuki describes it this way: "In the beginner's mind there are many possibilities, [but] in the expert's
mind there are few."[6] To create from a place of beginner's mind
is to delight in not knowing, allowing ourselves to play, take
risks, and be surprised by what emerges. Often thought of as a
childlike state, to be in beginner's mind is to drop any expectations of outcome, and with it, the shame and embarrassment
that so often surface in adulthood, which can inhibit us from
experimenting with something new, or even something familiar
in a new way. To say that God created the world "with beginner's mind" is to lift up an image of a playful, curious God who
creates as a process of growth, discovery, and delight—thereby
inviting us to do the same.

Pause for a moment and see if you can remember back
to when you first heard of "God." What image comes to mind?
Chances are it's not one of a playful, irreverent, curious deity.
At best, most of us were offered images of God more in line
with Rashi's all-powerful master of the cosmos, which came
along with the additional attributes of anger, remoteness,

6   Shunryū Suzuki, *Zen Mind, Beginner's Mind* (New York: Weatherhill, 1970), 21.

jealousy, and domination. This is an image of a God who violently carries out His will upon His subjects (it goes without saying that this image of God was always "He"). For this God, creation is a step-by-step series of commands enacted upon inert material. And if we believe that we are made in that image, we also might behave as domineering, dogmatic rulers on earth. Yet, as we've been exploring, this isn't the only way to view God. Far from it. How might we understand the creation of the universe—and ourselves—differently if we imagine God as creating with beginner's mind?

Jewish tradition teaches that "God spoke and the world came into being."[7] And as we read in Genesis, *"Vayomer Elohim yehi or,"* "God said, 'Let there be light,' and there was light."[8] Throughout the opening verses of Genesis, again and again, God says *"vayehi,"* "let there be," referring to light, land, oceans, animals, peoples—and then there was. In the view of the all-powerful master, God is a sole actor requiring no relationship or assistance in these successive stages of creation. This God acts as if His will alone, exerted upon mute matter, is all that really matters. There is no ambiguity or collaboration in this narrative. God is an isolated expert, successfully executing a precise plan.

However, as we are created in the image of the Creative force itself, we can call forth other images of the Divine. When we look again at these verses with beginner's mind, there is an opportunity for us to view this word *"vayehi"* from another vantage point. While the word *"vayehi"* can be interpreted as an order for something to exist ("there shall be"), this reading flattens the creative process and removes all relationality, nuance, and serendipity. This interpretation also excludes us from recognizing ourselves in this process of Creation. Outside of fairy tales and fantasy, no mortal creature can make a snap command that then immediately comes into being.

---

7 Psalms 33:9.
8 Genesis 1:3.

I want something more from the text—something that honors the aliveness of the world, that lifts up the interconnection between me and everything I touch in a mysterious but thrilling dance of creation. And if I want something more, why would God want anything less?

I imagine a God who approaches the raw elements of creation with a beginner's mind, and allows previously imperceptible possibilities to reveal themselves. And indeed, when approached from a different angle, the very same text suggests the possibility of a God who creates from a place of openness and spontaneity—with a beginner's mind. Rather than a command given from on high, what if instead we read *"vayehi"* the way we might in English, as an affirmation of what is, or even as a reverent blessing laced with delight. What if instead of a directive "let there be!" God's *"vayehi"* is simply an act of letting it be—noticing and welcoming the articulation and formation of a new reality as it emerges? We might imagine God "fluttering over the face of the deep," as the text says, noticing flickers of light amid the darkness, like phytoplankton glowing in the inky sea at night. God beholds what is, the glimmers that are appearing on their own, and in a dance of call and response, welcomes them to come more fully into existence: *"Vayehi*—let it be."

It is good

Surprised and delighted by what has arisen, God pauses to appreciate the various phases and fruits of the cosmic creative process, exclaiming again and again: *"Ki tov*—it is good." In our own creative process, what does it mean for something to be "good"? Often this word is used to designate a judgment by a recognized authority: teachers, art critics, parents, and peers. The accolade of "good" is most often used to describe the final product, while the *process* of creating is often hidden from sight. In this rereading, however, God creates with a beginner's mind, which privileges process over final product. Spontaneous, improvisational, open, and receptive. This is the creative process that we can access at any moment. When we, like God, are able to approach the elements present in our lives with a beginner's mind, we become aware of the inherent goodness and aliveness in all things, and notice that they engage us in a collaborative call and response. *Ki tov* — it is good to see things fresh, to welcome new interpretations, to let what is emerging reveal itself, and to witness the perpetual motion of our creative process with joy and reverence.

With wisdom

In addition to understanding the first word of the Torah, *beresheit*, as meaning that God created the world with a beginner's mind, we can turn to the rabbis and Kabbalists for a host of novel interpretations of this unique word and its significance. One method used by the sages to derive new commentary was to link two verses from different places in Jewish sacred text together through a word that appears in both, applying the meaning found in one verse to the other. Looking to other places where the word *resheit* is used, the rabbis found the phrase "*resheit chochmah*," "the beginning of wisdom," in Psalms, establishing a connection between the word *resheit* (as in *beresheit*) and the concept of wisdom.[9] They also turned to Proverbs and the verse, "*Adonai bechochmah yesod aretz*," "with wisdom God formed the foundation of the earth," explicitly naming that wisdom was present and involved in the beginnings of creation.[10] Rather than reading this as saying, "God, in God's wisdom, formed the earth," Beresheit Rabbah, a collection of midrashim on the book of Genesis, reads "wisdom" not as a quality but as a character in the

9   Psalms 111:10.
10 Proverbs 3:19.

creation story.[11] And in the eighth chapter of Proverbs, which is
written in the voice of *Chochmah*, Wisdom is portrayed as an
entity that existed prior to creation, alongside God. In the text,
Wisdom says, "I was there when God set the heavens into
place…When God fixed the foundations of the earth, I was with
God as a confidant, a source of delight every day."[12] Not alone,
but rather in partnership with Wisdom, the proverb suggests,
God created the world. Even before the divine creative process
began, according to this text, the primordial force of Wisdom
already existed—and she was a dear friend and companion
to God. Reading this interpretation back into the *beresheit* of
Genesis, the opening line of Torah can be understood as saying
something like, "in collaboration with Wisdom, God created
the world." Drawing insight for our own creative process from
this interpretation of God's creation of the world suggests not
only that we don't have to go it alone, but that collaboration
and partnership are key elements of creation.

The question of why God created the world has been
fodder for countless commentators over the centuries. One
answer given by the sages is that God created the world
because there was not yet anyone to witness or praise God's
actions.[13] In other words: God created out of a sense of
loneliness. In some ways, this interpretation resonates.
If God is an all-powerful master—the solitary ruler, apart
and distinct from His subjects—why wouldn't God be lonely?
Yet, what expansive possibilities might be opened up if we
see the Divine as creating not from a feeling of loneliness,
but rather from a place of joy and connection, in partnership
with Wisdom? Perhaps the experience of creativity in partnership is itself an antidote to the feelings of loneliness that
pervade contemporary society. We might imagine that
not only do we human beings benefit from a good *chavruta*,

11 Beresheit Rabbah 1:1.

12 Proverbs 8:27, 8:29–30.

13 Pirkei deRabbi Eliezer 3.

but so does God! In the immense task of creating the world, God had Wisdom as a collaborator and, together, they supported, inspired, and delighted each other in the dynamic flow of the creative process.

The creative process doesn't have to be lonely, as it can sometimes feel. Instead, it can open us up to a loving, playful, generous awareness that precedes and underlies everything and, whether we are by ourselves or with others, is always available to cocreate with us. There is much more available to us — within ourselves and in the universe — than might be readily apparent. Creativity emerges not only through our use of tangible tools and materials — brush, paint, canvas, guitar, notebook, or pen — but also through unseen energies, like the ever-present wisdom of the universe, that are there to buoy and aid us. In this rabbinic retelling, we are reminded that none of us, not even God, does anything alone. Can we let ourselves believe that there is an underlying wisdom and generative energy that we can access? Can we feel wisdom constantly flowing towards and through us, feeding our imagination and fertilizing our visions so they take root? When things feel overwhelming, like it's all on our shoulders, it can be comforting and strengthening to under-stand creation as a loving partnership, sustained by ongoing playful collaboration with forces that are larger than ourselves.

But what is wisdom, exactly? In a deft poetic maneuver, the Zohar offers a surprising answer to this question based on a creative reading of *chochmah*, the Hebrew word for wisdom, by breaking the word into its two constituent syllables: *koach*, meaning "power," and *mah*, meaning "what."[14] In this reading, *chochmah* is the power of the question "what?" As in: "What is this? What else could it be?"[15] This interpretation suggests that wisdom is not born from facts and answers, but rather from the creative potential of curiosity and questioning.

---

14 Zohar, Numbers 220b.
15 Gratitude to Estelle Frankel for her beautiful book *The Wisdom of Not Knowing*, where I first learned this piece of Zohar.

Expanding this idea further, the Zohar derives another perspective on *chochmah* from a verse in the book of Job. In the traditional reading, the verse says, "*vehachochmah, me'ayin timatzeh*"—"wisdom, from where can it be found?"[16] The Zohar, however, plays with the word "*ayin*," which means "where" but can also be translated as "nothingness": "Wisdom, from nothingness, is found."[17] Wisdom, in this reading, arises from a place of fertile spaciousness, of curiosity and inquiry, and a sense of infinite possibility. The Divine, in whose image we are made, can hold both the wild, teeming multiplicity of life and the empty void all at once. When we tap into our inner wisdom, we too can find the strength, curiosity, and patience required to sit with the unknown, and remain open long enough for what wants to come next to arise.

---

16 Job 28:12.
17 Asher ben David, quoted in Daniel C. Matt, *The Essential Kabbalah: The Heart of Jewish Mysticism* (San Francisco: HarperSanFrancisco, 1995), 66.

בראשית ברא אלהים את השמים ואת הארץ.

Beresheit bara Elohim et hashamayim ve'et ha'aretz.

IN THE BEGINNING [WITH BEGINNER'S MIND] GOD CREATED HEAVEN AND EARTH.
GENESIS 1:1

Beginner's Mind　BERESHEIT　בראשית

The Torah begins with the word *beresheit*. Often translated as "in the beginning" or "as God began," another way we might interpret *beresheit* is "with beginner's mind." The opening words of the Torah could then be read as: "With a beginner's mind, God created the world."

To approach something with a beginner's mind is to revisit something that feels well-known or familiar and set aside our expectations and preconceived ideas in order to rediscover it anew, like a beginner. Just as God creates the world with a beginner's mind, so too can we, who are made in the divine image, create from a place of openness and curiosity, whether we are making art, innovating in our professional lives, coming together in new ways across differences, processing grief and challenges, or any of the myriad ways we create and recreate ourselves and the world we share together.

Materials needed

A piece of paper and any writing or drawing supplies.

Prompts

↝ Can you imagine God creating with a beginner's mind? What does this evoke for you? Does it feel unsettling? Exciting? Something else?

↝ Consider *chochmah* as an energy — mysterious, undefinable — that propels God to begin creating the world. Have you ever felt compelled to begin creating something (e.g., a business, a piece of art, a community group)? If so, what was the origin of that feeling? A dream? A chance conversation? An emergent need? A question?

↝ Have you ever collaborated on a creative project with someone who you felt was supportive and in tune with your process? What was that experience like?

↝ Often when we create things, we have a guidebook to follow (e.g., furniture assembly instructions, a recipe, a craft project). Can you think of a time when you had to begin something without any specifications or clear plan? What did you do? To whom or to what did you turn?

Write or draw your responses to these prompts and include any other reflections that follow.

Reflection

Core to the creative process is the oscillation between being stirred up and allowing ourselves to settle down, between intuition and intellect, between taking in new information and seeing where this information lands in our own lived experience. Notice where you are at this moment. What feels alive? Unsettling? Exciting? Unclear?

והארץ היתה **תהו ובהו** וחשך על-פני תהום
ורוח אלהים מרחפת על-פני המים.

*Veha'aretz haytah **tohu vavohu** vechoshekh al penei tehom
veruach Elohim merachefet al penei hamayim.*

AND THE EARTH WAS **CHAOS AND VOID**, WITH DARKNESS ON THE FACE OF THE DEEP,
AND A BREATH OF GOD FLUTTERING UPON THE FACE OF THE WATERS.
GENESIS 1:2

Creation Comes from Chaos and Void

According to many rabbinic commentaries and philosophies across cultural traditions, the world was created *ex nihilo* — from nothing. We are taught that God is so powerful that God was able to create the entire universe out of thin air — or rather, out of the void before air was even created. Yet, if we look more closely at the opening lines of the creation story, we can see that before God began creating, much already existed. The second verse of Genesis reads, "The earth was chaos and void (*tohu vavohu*), with darkness on the face of the deep, and a breath of God fluttering upon the face of the waters."[1] In the beginning, there was this cosmic womb of the world: darkness and depth, chaos and void, water, wind, and the breath of the Divine. The world began from the swirling depths, full of creative energy, the place of all possibilities and no guarantees. A bubbling cauldron of starlight and galaxies, life and death, ancestors and future generations, in which swims the seed of all that will ever be — every imaginable future contained within in its cells, macrocosmic potentialities compressed, as if by magic, into microcosmic miniature.

---

1   Genesis 1:2.

Primordial elements

Before creation began, primordial elements existed. Using these raw materials, God created the world. A beautiful midrash on the creation of the world brings this interpretation to life through an argument between a philosopher and Rabban Gamliel, the leading rabbinic authority of his time: seeking to discredit the God of Torah, the philosopher challenges Rabban Gamliel, saying that God may be a great artist, but surely God's greatness was made possible by the materials God used to create the world. What were those materials? The philosopher replies, "Chaos, void, darkness, water, wind, and the depths."[2] In the context of this text, the philosopher is challenging the notion of God's ultimate power, in essence saying: sure, God enacted an incredible feat in bringing forth the world, but it really wasn't all that remarkable because God had such an array of materials on hand to work with.

Perhaps Rabban Gamliel was offended at this seemingly dismissive attitude towards God's omnipotence. But for us, this doesn't need to be an affront at all. Instead, the philosopher's words can empower us to use the raw materials that exist in our lives—half-formed thoughts, unclear emotions, nascent ideas—in our own creative process. In this story, rather than striving for something pristine and completely separate from anything that had existed before, God works with what is already available. In the process of creation, God turns to what is present and finds abundance. Rather than being seen as undesirable elements that stand in the way of creation, God embraces the darkness, depths, chaos, and void as generative. And, as human beings made in God's image, we can too.

---

2   Beresheit Rabbah 1:9.

Working with the stuff of our lives

In our own lives, simply finding the time or right conditions to tap into our creativity can be a challenge. But what if, instead of believing that there will be some perfect moment when the chaos and void of our lives will subside, we could recognize that every moment, brimming with chaos and void, is, in fact, the perfect moment? What if we allowed the messy stuff of our lives to fuel, inspire, and be transformed through our creative process? Just as God reached into the primordial elements that existed prior to creation, each of us contains chaos, void, and darkness in our depths. When I engage in any creative process— be it a piece of writing, or putting together a weekday dinner for my family—my first impulse is often to look outside myself to find what I think I need to make it happen. Depending on the day and the task, this might mean a clear head, more free time, a better computer, an additional skill, or, in the case of dinner, perhaps a takeout menu—the list goes on. I often plan to get started just as soon as I take care of all these other issues, imagining that once they get resolved, I'll be ready and prepared to begin.

All of those things that arise in my mind as necessities may indeed be wonderful to have, or important to address, and it's true that, depending on the project, some amount of time, space, or supplies may be needed. At the same time, I've found that my creative process is most nourishing when I bring whatever is alive for me in the moment to what I am doing, including my frustration with the conflicts, stresses, and deficiencies of everyday life. Creative processes of all kinds can be a way to work with what we've got and allow whatever is there for us—the pleasant and the not so pleasant, the clear and the muddled, the familiar and the strange—to serve as the raw materials for the act of creating. As we become immersed in our process, we give ourselves the chance to enter into a flow state in which our thinking mind has a chance to quiet, the stress and distractions of our lives recede, and things can begin to open and shift.

Our creative process provides a fertile space for feelings and physical sensations to unfold.

Like God, our challenge is to find the beauty of the materials on hand, the primordial chaotic stuff of our life — longing, questions, grief, confusion — and to create from here. The creative process beckons us to return to our depths, the chaos within. Our partnership with the Divine and our own inner wisdom give us the courage of spirit, intrepidness of mind, and openness of heart to notice what's there, to embrace its unique beauty and let it lead us to create something new.

The compost heap of creativity

In another fascinating midrash, the rabbis compare *tohu vavohu*, the "chaos and void" at the start of creation, to (of all things!) a pile of trash. This midrash brings a parable to help us understand the way these elements were viewed by the sages at that time. It reads:

> *Just as a king builds a palace in a place of sewers, dunghills, and garbage, everyone who says: "This palace is built on sewers, dunghills, and garbage" discredits it, so too, everyone who says the world was created from "chaos and void" discredits it. Rabbi Hunna in the name of Bar Kafra said: If it were not written, we would not be able to say it, [but it says right there in the Torah!] "In the beginning God created" from what? "And the earth was chaos and void."*[3]

According to this midrash, one would never say about a king that he built his palace atop sewers and trash heaps; this would be disrespectful. Therefore, it would be all the more disrespectful to say that God created the world out

3   Beresheit Rabbah 1:5.

of these materials. The only reason we can say it without insulting God is that it's written right there in the Torah!

While some may see sewers, dunghills, and garbage as filthy refuse to be cleaned up and discarded, anyone who has spent time in a garden knows that what some consider waste, others recognize as rich nutrients to sustain ongoing life. The food scraps and cardboard we throw away while preparing dinner, when brought to the compost heap, over time, in the right conditions, transform into dark, rich soil, ready to feed the microorganisms, insects, and fungi that make the earth bloom. Sewers take away our waste so that it can be broken down; the water it travels in is treated to become drinkable and clear again. Rather than deriding the king in this story for building his palace on top of trash and decay, what if we celebrated his resourceful choice of location as symbolic of transformation and nourishment? What if rather than something shameful and disrespectful, we reframed the existence of what we currently consider "waste" as something necessary and generative? What if we stopped refusing our refuse?

To understand creation as originally arising from the refuse and decomposition of everything that came before is to see *everything* — even that which seems useless, repellent, or unsightly — as necessary parts of the whole. According to this reading, God relishes the mess and fecundity that accompany chaos and void because these are the raw materials from which everything emerges.

Waste becomes wonder

In her lecture "In Praise of *Tohu va-Vohu*," the psychologist and scholar Miriam Faust compares "the state of being 'unformed and void' that preceded Creation with a universal human state which is a precondition for the ability to create." Not only is it okay to say that chaos and void were the materials that God used to create the world, but in fact, these elements are essential to our lives and foundational to any creative process. To be unformed and void, Faust writes, is to "to 'break' and 'disorganize' the familiar picture of the world in order to free [oneself] from it and view reality in another way."[4]

To be in touch with our creativity is to see the potential in everything, especially in things we would normally see as a "mess" and try to clean up. The creative process can give us a hands-on experience of connection with and appreciation of *tohu vavohu*. Old envelopes, flowers that have withered and dried, fragments of objects found on the street, writing in our journal that appears rambling or nonsensical, mistakes we've made or noticed others making in the workplace, a string of notes that never made their way into a melody—things that we might at first think to toss away can be transformed into valuable gems. Through our energy and attention, what appears to be waste can become a wonder.

In our culture of disposability, the things that we throw away pile up in garbage dumps, or in the massive "garbage patches" that have accumulated in our oceans. But the pathway of *tohu vavohu* teaches us that through creativity, trash can be transformed into treasure. It's how we learn to acknowledge that we never really throw things away: that, in truth, there is no "away" for our "garbage." Whether literal or metaphorical, the things we regard as trash stay with us. The pathway of *tohu vavohu* invites us to work with what we have—both the beautiful and the broken, the repellent and the resplendent. The chaos and mess that we encounter in the world, and that we find within ourselves, are abundant raw materials waiting to be transformed and put to use in a new way. If we don't find a use for it, like the garbage patches floating in our seas, this material can accumulate in our psyche and soul, impeding the healthy flow of energy and blocking renewed inspiration. To live vibrant and full lives, we must be willing to encounter,

---

4   Miriam Faust, "In Praise of Tohu va-Vohu," lecture for Bar-Ilan University's Parshat Hashavua Study Center, October 18, 2014.

befriend, and eventually transform the refuse of our lives—to see it all as raw material for our own creative process of becoming.

In addition to trying to dispose of these elements, another response we often have to *tohu vavohu* is to turn away and deny its existence. It can feel deeply uncomfortable to be amid chaos and void, whether in the realm of ideas or in our actual lives. Rather than avoiding, or on the other end, attempting to fix, change, or beautify something that is difficult, what if we simply allow ourselves to encounter it as we can bear it—perhaps for brief moments at a time, humbly noticing our own limitations and returning again when we are able? For chaos and void to yield their wisdom and beauty, it often takes staying with the discomfort long enough for it to shift, change, and open to us. When I think about my own creative process, sometimes this looks like a jumble of words written on the page, a blur of unrefined shapes on the canvas, or a feeling pulling on me that I can't quite articulate. In each of these experiences I feel frustrated, unclear, and out of control. Yet, when I'm able to accept that confusion and return again the next day, or even the next hour, at some point the words begin to flow into something meaningful, the shapes start to cohere in a way that feels pleasing, the thoughts begin to come into focus and new insight emerges. Returning over and over to our work signifies a commitment to our creative process and a trust that it will unfold in its own time, through this oscillation of engagement and disengagement. This nurtures the relationship between ourselves, the materials, the ideas we are trying to engage, and the Creative Source itself, which is supporting us in this endeavor. As we enter into a relationship with the chaos and void—no longer something scary to be resisted or avoided—we can invite it to come forward and offer us its gifts.

Fluttering over the face of the deep

It's rarely ever comfortable or easy to stay in a place of not-knowing. Often, to quell our anxiety, we move to take action before we, or the situation at hand, are ready. We may feel like it's better to *do something (anything!)* rather than simply pause and wait until more clarity comes, trusting the timeframe of our own intuition arising. When we feel the urgency to "do something," or even to "just get started already," the story of God's creative process can remind us that pausing before taking action is actually a powerful act in and of itself.

The first verb in the Torah to describe divine action is *bara*, meaning "create," and the second is *merachefet*, meaning "flutter or hover." After describing the watery depths of creation as "chaos and void," the Torah refers to "a breath [wind or spirit] of God *fluttering* upon the face of the waters." The first creative move God makes is to flutter, gently, over the chaos and void, the darkness and deep waters. In most retellings of the creation story, this act of hovering is casually skipped over, as if it had no relevance to the grand tale of the cosmos. The story is told as if God's speech, as recounted in the famous first utterance, "let there be," is the primary action that brings the world into being. Yet, no rays of light or formation of words would have been possible without this initial creative act of fluttering. The opening lines of the creation story give us a powerful model of God staying with *what is* so that it can transform into *what could be*.

To flutter is to inhabit a liminal space between movement and stasis, generating the energy for something new to emerge. To paraphrase a teaching of the sixteenth-century biblical commentator Rabbi Ovadia ben Jacob Sforno, God's hovering was an act that "activated the atmosphere."[5] Here, above the primordial waters, we might imagine the divine energetic

---

5   Rabbi Ovadia ben Jacob Sforno on Genesis 1:2 in Eliyahu Munk, *HaChut haMeshulash* (Jerusalem: Ktav Publishing House, 2003). "Activated the atmosphere" is Munk's translation.

vibration like the rapid back and forth movements of a hummingbird's wings. The air begins to circulate, the waters start to ripple, and the landscape begins to come alive through this small, yet significant, movement.

It was this first act of *merachefet*—coming into resonance before taking any decisive action—that opened the doors to the creative process. Rather than a posture of avoidance or passivity, the act of fluttering in place takes discipline, coordination, effort, and focus. After encountering the jumble of primordial elements, rather than immediately beginning to move or make anything, God instead hovers in place, remaining in relationship with the magnificent mess of what is, until the next step becomes clear.

This initial stage of hovering, of fluttering in the liminal space before doing, can be a challenge in our lives—whether making art, navigating relationships, or in our professional work. We may experience an urge to "produce" without a clear sense of how to proceed, and this gap can create a sense of anxiety. This moment between inspiration and action is often unsettling, and our minds tend to wander. For most of us, ambiguity is destabilizing and often unnerving. The desire to skip over this stage is natural. Yet, Torah teaches that it is our ability to inhabit this moment of uncertainty that eventually allows our creative energy to flow and our process to unfurl. What would it mean for us to hover over the face of the chaos and void in our art, or our work, or our life? To gently, yet decisively, flutter our wings while remaining in place, alive and awake to the present moment, whatever it is, unafraid of the disarray?

When we stay in relationship with something, it changes, and so do we. Sustained attention, lightly held, allows things to shift. When we are able to be both present and open, things that once appeared intractable begin to reveal new possibilities. This practice of *merachefet* is something we can draw on when facing difficulty in our personal lives as well. For instance, imagine receiving a frustrating or upsetting email that was entirely unexpected; in this case, we would be well-served to exercise the discipline of *merachefet*—to "stay above it," so to speak—rather than "diving in," and immediately responding with a heated reply. Composing that heated reply could be part of our creative process, but rather than actually sending it, we might instead let it cool off in our drafts folder. In this way we remain in the place of *merachefet*, not denying our feelings or initial response, but allowing time and space for a deeper process to unfurl. When we give ourselves over to this stage of the creative process, there is always an element of surprise— something reveals itself that couldn't have been predicted.

In my own life, art-making has become a low-stakes way for me to practice this act of *merachefet*. I am reminded of a process I went through to create a particular painting. I covered the background with various colors and then began putting shapes on top, continuing to add color and form, until at some point I looked up and all I saw was a chaotic mess on the page. I felt embarrassed to look at what I had created. I hated what I saw and wanted to turn away, to start a new piece. Yet, I resolved to stay with it, to experiment with *merachefet*, to see what this approach could offer. I gazed at the piece; I walked around the room to view it from different angles; I stayed with my discomfort and let these emotions wash over me. After a few minutes, something began to shift. Shame and judgment started to give way to curiosity. My eye was drawn to a particular area in the piece; small, down in the corner, that intrigued me and seemed to call out for something more. I began adding small blue circles on top of the reddish orange shapes, and as I did so, my energy began to return. For hours, I was engrossed in what I was creating. Suddenly, the piece wasn't trash to be thrown away, but rather an entity of its own, calling out for care and attention to bring it more fully into being.

In the case of my painting, the act of attentively remaining with what *was* (as opposed to what *could be,* or what *could have been*) moved something internally for me, reactivating the atmosphere, allowing me to return to the energetic excitement of when I first began the painting. The shame, self-doubt, and self-criticism began to give way to curiosity and excitement. Just as Sforno interpreted God's hovering as a crucial stage of the world's creation, for all of us, this act of *merachefet* is a key to maintaining a relationship to anything we are working on that feels challenging, stagnant, or unclear.

We can be so quick to judge ourselves, so keen on getting rid of any evidence of our ignorance or inexperience. We can easily get overwhelmed by the chaos and void, afraid of what it reflects back to us, of what it might call forth from us. Not only that, but our culture's emphasis on productivity often devalues this kind of uncertainty; we internalize the notion that working without a specific goal or outcome is "wasting" time. Here, we can draw inspiration from God's example: not rushing into action, not needing to instantaneously produce or fix anything, but rather just being present and observing what is, with all of the discomfort this may bring. Simply staying present in this way allows what's there to let us know what's needed next.

The breath of God

One practice that can help us slow down enough so we can engage in this act of "hovering" is to connect to our breath. In the verse in Genesis that we've been looking at in this section, it is "the breath of God" (*ruach Elohim*) that flutters over the elements. The meaning of this Hebrew phrase is reflected in the English word "inspire": the origin of the word is the Latin *inspirare*, meaning "to blow or breathe into," from *spirare,* meaning "to breathe."[6] Inspiration is defined as "the process that takes place when somebody sees or hears something that causes them to … want to create something."[7] This perfectly describes the *ruach Elohim merachefet* — the breath of God that

6 "Breathing Life Into 'Inspire,'" *Merriam-Webster* online, accessed January 26, 2024.
7 "Inspiration," *Oxford Learner's Dictionaries* online, accessed February 2, 2024.

flutters above the waters, opening the way for inspiration to arise. Sometimes all we need to do is feel our breath within us in order to slow down and encounter the world as it is, ourselves as we are. From this pregnant pause, a spark of inspiration can be born.

It is this very breath of God, the *ruach Elohim*, fluttering above the depths in the pause before creation, that is blown into human beings (*adam*) later on in the process of creation, as described in Genesis.[8] Shaped from the ground, molded from the red clay of the earth, humans emerge from the primordial elements as a combination of earthly dust and divine breath. God's outbreath becomes our inbreath, and our outbreath becomes the inbreath of the plankton, plants, and trees. When we recognize the grandeur of something as subtle as our breath, we know ourselves to be interwoven with and a necessary part of all of creation. To pause, even briefly, and consciously connect to our breath is itself an act of fluttering or hovering over the miracle of the moment we're in.

Breath is a constant, ever-flowing embodied reminder that we are interconnected with all of creation. It can also remind us that this ever-present, creative life force flows through us, even at times when the weight of the world can make it hard to breathe. The late eighteenth-century Hasidic master Rebbe Nachman of Breslov teaches us, "If you want to return to God you must make yourself into a new creation. You can do this with a sigh."[9] And what is a sigh but a release of all the breath we've been holding? We sigh and surrender to "what is" right now—to this moment, in all its chaos and void, its possibility and pain. We release all that we've been holding in, holding out for, holding on to, holding up. As we let the stale air out, we breathe into what's here for us, shimmering in the present, right here, right now. As Rebbe Nachman teaches: "Every exhalation is the death of the moment that has passed,

8   Genesis 2:7.
9   Rabbi Nachman of Breslov, *Chayei Moharan* 37.

in preparation for the birth of the new moment," and in this way, we are able to continually release ourselves from the old and open ourselves "to receive new vitality."[10] Just as God's tremulous breath above the chaos and void activates the atmosphere and stirs inspiration, so too does our own breath open us to the universe moving through us, creating ourselves anew with each revitalizing inhalation and softening sigh.

---

10 Breslov, *Chayei Moharan* 37. See also, Avraham Greenbaum, "Teshuva — Returning to God," The Essential Rabbi Nachman, Azara Institute, 2007.

בראשית ברא אלהים את השמים ואת הארץ:

Beresheit bara Elohim et hashamayim ve'et ha'aretz:

WHEN GOD BEGAN CREATING HEAVEN AND EARTH

והארץ היתה **תהו ובהו** וחשך על פני
תהום ורוח אלהים מרחפת על פני המים.

*Veha'aretz haytah **tohu vavohu** vechoshekh al penei tehom veruach
Elohim merachefet al penei hamayim.*

AND THE EARTH WAS **CHAOS AND VOID**, WITH DARKNESS ON THE FACE OF THE DEEP,
AND A BREATH OF GOD FLUTTERING UPON THE FACE OF THE WATERS.
GENESIS 1:1–2

Creation Comes from Chaos and Void   TOHU VAVOHU   תהו ובהו

When we consider the creation of the world, we often imagine
it as being created from nothing. Yet, in Genesis we read
that the earth was "*tohu vavohu*" (chaos and void) before God's
creative process even began. In the creation of the world, chaos
and void are the raw elements of creation, along with water,
darkness, and breath. God flutters over the depths of chaos
and void, inviting these elements to transform into land, stars,
animals, plants, and human beings. Ancient Jewish wisdom
teaches that each human being is a world unto ourselves.
Within each one of us there exist elements of chaos and void—
the raw materials of creation. Just as God transforms the
tohu vavohu of the world, each of us is invited to work with all
that is unresolved or unclear within ourselves and to transform what we find into what we seek.

Materials needed

The "junk drawer" in your house; a piece of paper and pen.

Prompt

Go to the "junk drawer" in your home. You know the place—where rubber bands, old batteries, lip balm, birthday candles, old letters, and all manner of odds and ends accumulate. Open the drawer and explore the contents of what is there. Spend five minutes writing in response to what comes up, letting all judgments, memories, associations, and feelings onto the page. Now ask yourself: What are three actions I could take regarding these items? For example, you could tidy up the drawer and throw some things out, or arrange these objects into a pleasing design on the table, or write a poem inspired by one of them. Pick any one of the actions you brainstorm, and follow where it leads for the next ten minutes. Take your time, follow your intuition, but stay in contact with the items. At the end of your process, write a reflection in response to your experience.

Reflection

In this exercise you worked with the jumble of material found in a junk drawer.

↝   What did it feel like to encounter this place of chaos in your home or office? Overwhelming? Amusing? Surprising? Something else?

↝   What did you notice when you first opened the drawer? Were you pleased? Inspired? Anxious?

↝   How did you choose to work with what was there? How did it feel to do so?

↝   Returning to the concept of *tohu vavohu*, what (if anything) arose for you in relation to this text from this experience?

↝   How might the concept of creating from *tohu vavohu* be helpful for you in your life? What chaos and void within you, or in the world, might you seek to transform?

The Place of All Possibility

ויאמר יהוה אל-אברם **לך-לך** מארצך
וממולדתך ומבית אביך אל-הארץ אשר אראך.

Vayomer YHVH *el Avram **lekh lekha** me'artzekha*
umimoledetekha umibeit avikha el ha'aretz asher arekha.

AND GOD SAID TO AVRAM, "**GO FORTH** FROM YOUR LAND, FROM YOUR BIRTHPLACE
AND FROM YOUR PARENTS' HOUSE, TO THE LAND THAT I WILL SHOW YOU."
GENESIS 12:1

We Are Called to Journey into the Unknown

Among the most quintessential stories in Jewish tradition is that of God's call to Avraham, the first biblical patriarch: "*Lekh lekha*," which is commonly translated as "go forth." The rest of the line continues, "From your land, from your birthplace and from your parent's house, to the land that I will show you."[1] With this call, Avraham is directed to leave his origins behind — all that he knows, and who he has been up to this point in his life — and venture out into the unknown to discover who he will be and to bring blessing to the world. Over the course of his journey, he will face challenges big and small; his identity will shift and change; and he will come into a deeper relationship with himself, with others, and with God. A willingness to venture forth into the unknown is foundational to any creative process. When we heed the call to journey beyond the limits of what we currently understand, something new can come through us into the world.

A voice calls out to each of us
We might begin with the question, as many sages do: Of all people to be called to this sacred mission, why Avraham? Though he is now regarded as the first Hebrew patriarch,

---

1 Genesis 12:1.

at the moment in which he is called by God in the Torah, there doesn't seem to be anything particularly special about him. In fact, there is so little detail pointing to why he is chosen that the rabbis invented countless midrashim to help explain why he, specifically, received the call of *lekh lekha*. Some commentators emphasize Avraham's uniqueness, imagining stories about his strong leadership qualities and brilliant mind. Others, however, suggest that Avraham deserved to receive the call precisely because he was just like the rest of us—he was unique and special in the way that all of us are unique and special. In this view, a call from God is not something reserved for the select few, but rather, it is for each and every one of us who choose to hear it.

To see ourselves as Avraham is to know that there is a voice that calls out constantly to each of us, urging us to venture into the unknown, and leave behind the comfort of what we know. This is the creative process of our lives. It is a process that began long before we were born, and will ripple out into the world for generations to come. We are each here in this life to bring forth something unique, that the world needs from each of us, and that we need for ourselves. Who we are and where we come from, our unique background and experiences, makes each of our journeys necessary for the full realization of the world. Creativity is how we tend and befriend that call—how we come to know it intimately and become able to carry it out.

A glimpse into my lekh lekha

For me, the call of *lekh lekha* was loudest during my last year of college—but it still took me some time to hear it, and then to really listen. Throughout college I was intensely focused on my studies, thinking that I wanted to go into academia once I graduated. My area of focus was environmental studies and anthropology—I wanted to understand humans, why and how we did things, and how we could get ourselves to live in ways that were more sustainable. All of my studies and activities during college—from running the student environmental organization to a semester abroad studying coral populations—were focused on this goal.

But I began to notice a deep emptiness at my core, an aching for something beyond the life I was living. At the same time, Jewish practices like prayer and Shabbat observance, which hadn't been central to my life since childhood, became important to me again. I had an urge to relearn the prayers I had known as a child, and so I got myself a traditional *siddur* (prayer book) and started teaching myself how to use it. I began cooking Shabbat meals and inviting my friends, none of whom were practicing Jews, to light the candles and accompany me in saying the traditional Shabbat prayers. I stopped going out on Friday nights, even when it meant celebrating Shabbat at home alone. I had no idea how any of this fit in with my future plans; it just felt, somewhat inexplicably, like what I needed to do.

It was during this time—when I began to notice the dissonance between the plans I had set out for myself and the growing desire to reconnect to my Jewish heritage—that I heard the call to become a rabbi. For me, this was a *lekh lekha* moment. At the time, I had no idea what this meant, what would be involved, or why I was being called. The idea felt, on one hand, obvious and clear, and thinking about it brought me excitement and relief. And yet on the other hand, this idea seemed totally bizarre, out of place, and terrifying. I hadn't taken one Jewish studies class in college, hadn't stepped foot into the Hillel building (the center of Jewish life on campus), and had no mentors or friends who had gone down this road. Despite all of this, I could feel inside myself that this was the path I was being called to travel.

Following this call was thrilling and painful all at once. Past dreams and goals fizzled as new ones began to emerge. The long-term relationship I was in ended. I moved across the country to work for the one rabbi I knew at the time who was doing work that I could imagine myself doing.[2] My atheist professor in the biology department wrote a recommendation letter for me when I applied to rabbinical school the next year. While it certainly is not as grand as Avraham's *lekh lekha*, in my own way, I was called to venture well beyond the life and lands I knew, into the unknown. That call came through a dissonant mix of discomfort and delight that showed me what else might be possible. It involved feelings of fear, confusion, loneliness, risk, and loss—but it also promised blessing on the other side. Heeding this call changed the course of my life forever, and I am so glad that I listened.

A new creation

In Genesis, heeding the call of *lekh lekha* leads to a profound transformation, and corresponding change of name— from Avram to Avraham. After enduring many hardships and challenges along his journey, God blesses Avraham with a new, expanded purpose and identity. In Hebrew, this new name is created by simply adding one letter, *hei* (equivalent to the English letter *h*). Why the letter *hei*? A Talmudic discussion on the creative significance of this letter says:

> *When the verse states: "These are the generations of the heaven and of the earth when they were created* [behibare'am]*"* *(Genesis 2:4), do not read it as* behibare'am, *meaning "when they were created"; rather, read it as* be'hei bera'am, *meaning "God created them with the letter* hei." *This verse demonstrates that the world was created with the letter* hei.[3]

2   Michael Lerner, founder of *Tikkun* magazine and Beyt Tikkun synagogue in the Bay Area.
3   Babylonian Talmud, Menachot 29b.

According to one commentary on this act of renaming,
by lending Avram a *hei*, by turning Avram into Avraham,
God was creating him anew.[4] To follow the call of *lekh lekha*
is to allow ourselves to be remade, linking ourselves back
to the creation of the world.

Avraham is not the only one whose name is changed.
His wife, Sarai, also receives a new name with the addition
of a *hei* (becoming Sarah) to show that she too is created anew.
Midrash teaches that when God told Avram that he would
bear a son from his wife, Sarai, Avram looked into the stars
and saw that he and his wife could not have any children.
God responded by telling him that while it was true that Avram
and Sarai could not have children, Avraham and Sarah could.[5]
In ancient Jewish thought, the stars represent "fixed" or "fated"
realities of life.[6] In this story, God lets Avram in on the secret
that exists beyond the stars, revealing the possibility of divine
intervention and radical transformation.

Notably, the letter *hei* is also one of the three letters in the
sacred and unpronounceable name of God, spelled *yud-hei-vav-hei*.
The addition of this letter to Avram and Sarai's names both
acknowledges and amplifies their connection to the Divine.
To go forth into the unknown is to open ourselves up to partnership with the infinite, and to allow for the possibility of a
radical shift in our life path and identity. As a quintessential
call of the creative process, this act of courageously going forth
into the unknown makes what was previously impossible possible in ways that can change the course of our future.

There are particular moments in our life when we can,
perhaps, hear this call more readily. We may imagine that
these are moments of courage and strength on our part, when
we feel most competent and confident in embarking on

4   Yedidiah Tiah Weil, Marbeh Lesaper on Pesach Haggadah, Magid
     (drawing on Midrash Rabbah 12:2).

5   Beresheit Rabbah 44:12; Rashi on Genesis 15:5.

6   "Ancient Jewish History: Astrology," Jewish Virtual Library,
     accessed February 8, 2024.

a new challenge. However, the Torah offers a different (perhaps even opposite) perspective. When Avram hears the call of *lekh lekha*, he is in a period of frustration, stagnation, and loss. His father, Terach, had just passed away.[7] His wife, Sarai, could not conceive, and the couple had no children.[8] At seventy-five years old, the life that he had hoped for no longer seemed possible.

Just a few verses before *lekh lekha*, we read that Sarai and Avram "set out together from Ur of the Chaldeans for the land of Canaan; but when they had come as far as Haran, they settled there."[9] The literal meaning of the phrase "settled there" (*vayeishvu sham*) is that they ceased traveling and set up camp in Haran. Yet in these words we also hear another meaning of "settle"—to accept or agree to something that is less than satisfactory. We can imagine Avram and Sarai, tired from the waiting and wandering, simply deciding to settle where they were on their journey.

It was precisely at this moment that Avram heard that generative call of *lekh lekha*—not when the map was well-marked and clear, but when he had given up on the journey altogether. He hears it in a place of stagnation, perhaps even frustration. *Lekh lekha* comes to remind us that nothing is final, that there is always the potential for change. Even when we have "settled" for something (and perhaps especially in these moments), there is a force in the universe calling us towards vitality and new life. It is from here—from that jumble of discontent and desire— that the Divine so often speaks.

---

7   Genesis 11:32.
8   Genesis 11:30.
9   Genesis 11:31.

Getting going

Calls rarely arrive fully articulated. While Avraham heard
God's voice speaking directly to him, in our own lives, this kind
of "call" into the unknown could show up as an unnamable
feeling inside us, an image from a dream, or a curiosity that
beckons us to the point of creative distraction. Have you ever
heard a call of this nature? Something potent and yet inchoate
that seemed to be asking you to drastically change your life
and set out for somewhere in search of something that doesn't
even have a name. How did you respond? Did you push the
feeling away? Discuss it with a friend? Doubt the call itself?
Say yes immediately?

These calls can come at any point in our lives, not only
when we're ready and able to answer them, but also when
we doubt our capacities, or when we feel too established and
accomplished to strike out anew again. We may be reluctant
to follow where the call beckons us. Even when we want to
go, when we long for something new, when we're unhappy
or unfulfilled where we are, obstacles both inner and outer can
seem insurmountable, and we are tempted to turn away and
busy ourselves with the life in front of us. The rabbis imagine
that God, in fact, had been calling out to Avraham for some
time, but it was only at that moment of *lekh lekha* that he was
able to hear and heed the call. We don't know what made
Avraham take action at this moment, but we do know that in
our own lives, it often isn't until years later that we can fully
discern the factors that went into a life-altering decision.

To glean more insight into Avraham's experience, we can
parse out God's words themselves to deepen our understanding of what he might have heard. *Lekh lekha* is made up of two
short, seemingly simple words, but commentators across the
generations have unearthed myriad understandings of this
phrase. The word *"lekh"* is the imperative form of the verb
"to go"—as in "go!" What has intrigued commentators is the
addition of the word *"lekha."* While *lekh* is a clear imperative
form, *lekha* is more ambiguous and could mean many things.

Though most often understood as a conjugation that means "to [or for] yourself," the second word in the phrase has also been read as a conjugation of the verb "to go," repeating the first word but with additional emphasis, as in *"lekh, lekh"*—that is, "go, *go!*" Written without vowels, the ancient text leaves open this possibility. In this reading, God's words express the sense of agitation and urgency that Avraham requires to *get going*. There are times for each of us when our careful considerations get in the way of necessary action.[10] Though it can be supremely uncomfortable and challenging, sometimes we are best served when we stop trying to figure it all out and just make a move!

  This is exactly what Avraham does. When we look at the Hebrew, his response is clear and simple: *"Vayeilekh Avram."* "And Avram went forth."[11] In this moment in his life, in this particular emanation of the call, Avraham hears, and he goes! We can imagine what Avraham may have been going through prior to this moment. If this call had indeed, as the rabbis postulated, been issuing forth for some time, perhaps Avraham had been in a stage of *merachefet*, the meditative hovering or fluttering that we discussed earlier. In this stage, he may have been sorting through his fears and misgivings from a place of trembling and anticipation, and only then, having done that work, could he let himself hear and really feel the urgency of this call. This reading can shed light on the different stages of the creative process, and the pathways to creativity that we have explored here, from *merachefet* to *lekh lekha* (or *lekh, lekh!*). Sometimes, setting off on a journey begins with a period of gestation and contemplation. Although it may be imperceptible to those around us, and less dramatic as the abrupt departure from home, this "hovering" is an essential aspect of heeding the call to face, and venture into, the unknown.

---

10 See, for example, "Lech Lecha: Leaving Your Comfort Zone," *Jewish Standard*, October 10, 2013.
11 Genesis 12:4.

Going within to go forth

The "get going" interpretation of God's command to Avraham is in contrast to Rashi, who (like many other commentators) reads the second word in this phrase as *lekha* ("to you" or "for you"). For Rashi, *lekha* here is understood as "for your benefit."[12] Rashi seems to recognize that though the journey may be difficult, and although we will undoubtedly encounter challenges along the way, there is something we need that this journey will provide. Rashi's reading teaches us that a meaningful quest is not necessarily about suffering and struggle, or exclusively for the good of others or even of the world. The root of any genuine call must authentically satisfy our own soul's purpose, to fulfill a need that we didn't know we had. When we recognize this, we understand that the things that bring us joy and truly light us up are the signposts on our path to a life of deep meaning. So often, we focus on the needs of others to the exclusion of our own desires, when in fact, Rashi seems to be saying, it is those things that delight and benefit our souls that allow us to contribute meaningful gifts to the world. The creative process is not a path of self-denial; it's a joyous comingling of that which is good for us, others, and the world.

The Hasidic masters, who understood all of Torah as a teaching about how to traverse our inner landscape, understand *lekha* slightly differently. In their interpretation, "to you" refers to the journey into yourself to become intimate with the spark of the Divine within. In this reading, God is commanding Avraham not only (or even primarily) to go out into the wider world beyond his "father's house," but rather to journey into the wilder world within.[13] There are times that require us to physically separate ourselves from the people and places we're familiar with in order to fully apprehend and follow

---

12 Rashi on Genesis 12:1.
13 This teaching is often attributed to Reb Nosson, a beloved student of Rebbe Nachman of Breslov.

our calling. At other times, our call may not require such a drastic physical separation. The real work is traveling into the deepest recesses of our heart to examine our most closely held beliefs, our suppressed longings, our untended griefs, even the principles and values that have guided our lives thus far. As the Hasidic masters often did, we can read God's command metaphorically. From this perspective, Avraham is being asked to leave behind not a physical land or place, but rather the values, beliefs, and principles that have been transmitted to him, perhaps without him even being aware of it.

The creative process is one of the ways we may take this internal journey. Through poetry, image, and metaphor we allow our inner landscape to become more vivid and clear. We journey into that landscape — sometimes with pleasure, other times with trepidation. The creative process provides us a low-stakes way of engaging in the generative oscillation between *merachefet* and *lekh, lekh* — when to settle and when to move. Sometimes we flee in frustration or discomfort, only to return the next day to receive clarity and insight. Even when circumstances prevent us from physically changing our place, the creative process opens a path for us to hear and respond to the *lekh lekha* call.

Going our own way

Drawing on the teachings of Rabbi Samson Raphael Hirsch (the nineteenth-century rabbi and intellectual founder of contemporary Orthodox Judaism), the scholar Rabbi Yosef Hershman opens up another vantage point on the meaning of the word *"lekha."* He writes, "If the principle adopted by the majority is untrue — then go it alone and serve [God]!"[14] In this reading, *lekh lekha* is a command to follow one's calling even

---

14 Rabbi Yosef Hershman, "Parshat Lech Lecha: Go It Alone," Ohr Somayach website, November 9, 2019.

when that means going against what is currently accepted. The inclusion of the word "*lekha*" serves to clarify the meaning of God's instruction to Avraham as "go your own way." Among others, Hirsch has argued that, for Avraham, this means establishing monotheism, the worship of one God as opposed to the polytheism prevalent at that time in ancient Mesopotamia.[15] When applied to our own lives, this may mean following our intuition and sense of integrity regardless of how that matches up with current trends or familial patterns. Tuning into one's own inner sense of what is right, and then putting that into action, can mean discomfort, uncertainty, unpopularity, and sometimes even personal risks to one's physical safety. But there is also immense potential for reward. Looking to the story of Avraham for courage and guidance, we might ask, what beauty, what blessing, what unimagined creations might emerge when we go our own way?

The creative act of following our own intuition can have positive consequences that ripple out into the wider world. As we practice recognizing, and honoring, our own deep knowledge and intuition, listening for the call that beckons us and following where it leads (even—especially—when that place is unclear, uncomfortable, or unknown), we develop within us the capacity to create positive social change and personal transformation. Many thinkers, from Albert Einstein to Audre Lorde, have pointed out that we need new tools, and new manners of thinking, to solve the problems that plague us. Perhaps what we need is to "go our own way," with an awareness and appreciation of what came before us, and a commitment to cross-pollinating our ideas with one another, so that we might open the possibility of a more resilient and resonant world.

---

15 Rabbi Dr. Joseph Breuer, *Introduction to Rabbi Samson Raphael Hirsch's Commentary on the Torah: Volume I* (New York: Philipp Feldheim, 1948), 43–44.

Seeking our roots

However, the *lekh lekha* journey is not *only* about looking towards the emerging future; it is also about coming to know our origins. The nineteenth-century Hasidic thinker Mordechai Yosef Leiner of Izbica, best known for his work *Mei haShiloach,* understands the meaning of *lekha* in the command *"lekh lekha"* as "go *to yourself,"* as in seek your own roots.[16] In this paradoxical interpretation, Avraham is instructed to leave behind his place of origin as a means to better understand where it is he comes from. Each of us are shaped by the places where we grow up, the households in which we're raised, the communities that we've been a part of. *Lekh lekha* is asking us to inquire into the stories, both told and untold, that formed and fueled the culture and home that grew us. What are the lineages, histories, traumas, joys, and legacies that underlie and form the backdrop of the lives we lead? It is only after leaving home that Avraham becomes better equipped to discern what of himself is actually his, what is his father's, and what comes from the soil in which he grew.

The creative process supports us in the work of reflecting on and unearthing the stories and ancestries that shape us. In the words of my mother, Pat B. Allen, creating "allows us to transcend linear time, to travel backward and forward into personal and transpersonal history, into possibilities that weren't realized and those that might be."[17] In a way, the creative process exists outside of time; it allows us access to a space in which we can traverse the past, present, and even the future. Here, through freewriting, imaginative reverie, and intuitive creating, we can try on alternative histories and ideas, conjure up images of those who came before us, and receive from our ancestors ways of carrying forward work that they began. Engaging in the creative process is a way of cultivating and reviving insights, customs, and wisdoms that have fallen

16 See Genesis 12:1 in *Mei haShiloach* (c. 1840–1860; Sifrei Izhbitza-Radzin: Bnei Brak, 2005).

17 Pat B. Allen, *Art Is a Spiritual Path: Engaging the Sacred through the Practice of Art and Writing* (Boston: Shambhala, 1995), 1–2.

into disuse; it widens the channel between realms. This call of *lekh lekha* invites us to encounter that place in ourselves where the past and the present meet, and where the once obscured aspects of our lives can now be seen.

Creative destruction

Avraham's relationship to his own roots feature in several midrashim about his personal journey. The rabbis have conjured many stories imagining the details of Avraham's early relationship to his father, Terach. In one such midrash, Terach owns a store that sells idols, where Avraham works as a young man (as one does in the family shop). As he grows up, Avraham begins to develop a relationship to the Divine that goes beyond these human-made idols. One day, Terach asks his son to mind the store. As the midrash goes, with Avraham alone in the shop:

> *A woman arrived, holding a plate of grain. She said to Avram, "Take this and offer it before them [to the idols]." Avram got up, took a stick in his hands and broke all the idols, leaving the stick in the hand of the largest one. When his father returned, he asked, "Who did this to them?" Avram answered, "What have I to hide? A woman came, carrying a plate of grain. She said to me, 'Take this and offer it before them.' I offered it before them, and this one here said, 'I shall eat first.' Then that one said, 'I shall eat first.' The largest idol got up, took the stick, and shattered them!" Terach said: "What nonsense are you telling me! Are they then conscious?" Avram answered, "Do your ears not hear what your lips are saying?"*[18]

In smashing the idols and confronting his father, Avraham is mocking and rejecting his inheritance. While we might extoll Avraham for confronting his father's idolatrous ways,

---

18 Beresheit Rabbah 38:13.

or condemn him for disrespecting his elders, we can also look at this story as a teaching about the creative process. We might imagine the satisfaction Avraham felt while smashing those idols. But the satisfaction of destroying an illusion is often followed by feelings of despair and cynicism when there's nothing more genuine or sustaining to replace it. We might judge ourselves for ever having believed something that now appears to us as obviously misguided or false. We may end up embittered and estranged from our family or our community, or from practices which now seem naïve and hollow. The creative process can be a repository for all of these complex and often forbidden feelings—the anger and despair, the heartache and loss, the sense of being betrayed by those we trusted—offering us some relief and distance from what otherwise might be overwhelming emotions. The creative process can provide space for acts of chaotic discharge, akin to Avraham's smashing of the idols. These acts can allow us to feel these feelings fully, to name and know them, and to release them, thereby reclaiming that energy for constructing new practices and beliefs. The pain and difficulty of such emotions is mitigated by the pleasure of making art—the pigment smearing onto the canvas, the inky intensity of the pen to the page, the way the air vibrates with the notes we sing. It is the release of these feelings that brings our body to a state of exhilaration and, eventually, relaxation and rest, freeing up energy for what comes next. It is from this state of awareness that acceptance and forgiveness can arise and something new can be born. For it is only when we give our discomfort the space it needs to express itself that these feelings can then shift and change—leading us beyond what we know.

In any creative process, we can rest assured in the knowledge that the "page" can hold it all. Whatever materials we are working with can handle whatever it is we are feeling—our most intense emotions, our biggest struggles, our deepest longings; all that may not be welcome in our daily lives can be received and transformed through the creative process.

Creating as a means of inquiring into all of these feelings
can be not only generative, but healing. Through our creative
process, we can explore what feels unclear in ourselves
and our lives, and make room for whatever is trying to emerge.
We do this not only for our own benefit, but to heal our connection to our roots as well — the people, places, practices, and
beliefs from which we came.

Sharing with others

Another midrash offers a multisensory metaphor for God's
words to Avraham. Prior to *lekh lekha*, the midrash says,
Avraham resembled a "bottle of perfume closed with a tight
fitting lid, lying in a corner so that its fragrant smell was
not spread. When it was moved, however, its fragrance was
spread."[19] Here, the *lekh lekha* journey grants Avraham the
spaciousness to develop new insights and beliefs — such as
faith in one god, which will become the basis for the earliest
iterations of Judaism — and to spread those ideas through
his travels. Like a fragrance, subtle and evocative at first, these
ideas grew in potency and attracted people to Avraham and
this new way of understanding the Divine.

   This unlikely metaphor gives us a delightful and oddly
feminine insight into the creative process: alluring, subtle,
drawn from the stuff of beautification and self-adornment, not
something to which we might expect a most beloved patriarch
would be compared. While the midrash seems to emphasize
the importance of the wafting perfume once the bottle is opened
and moved, we have an opportunity to honor the containment
of the stoppered bottle as well. Before any creative act begins,
there is usually something bubbling, brewing, churning inside
of us. In this phase, there aren't yet shapes or words to express
what this growing tension of half-formed thoughts and unclear

---

19 Beresheit Rabbah 39:2.

feelings means. "Keep a lid on it" is often an instruction to repress our feelings or thoughts, but what if we reimagined it as a vital part of the creative process and the *lekh lekha* journey? Here, "keeping a lid on it" could be understood as a way of containing, protecting, and developing these feelings and ideas more fully. At this point in the process, we're allowing our interior selves to gestate, as it were, until we are ready to express and share this part of ourselves. In the timeline of the creative process, at this moment we are creating just for ourselves, as an act of tender exploration. We protect what's emerging and do not submit ourselves to others' opinions or judgments, resisting the inclination to name, solve, share, or force something into the world prematurely—before it's ready, or before we are. The creative process urges us to trust that, as it was for Avraham, the stopper in the bottle of our perfume will be removed eventually, when the time is right, and when it is, what wafts forth will be fragrant, beautiful, and worthy of being spread.

ויאמר יהוה אל-אברם **לך-לך**
מארצך וממולדתך ומבית אביך אל-הארץ אשר אראך.

Vayomer YHVH *el Avram **lekh lekha***
me'artzekha umimoledetekha umibeit avikha el ha'aretz asher arekha.

AND GOD SAID TO AVRAM, "**GO FORTH** FROM YOUR LAND, FROM YOUR BIRTHPLACE AND
FROM YOUR PARENTS' HOUSE, TO THE LAND THAT I WILL SHOW YOU."
GENESIS 12:1

We Are Called to Journey into the Unknown   LEKH LEKHA   לך-לך

In Genesis (12:1–3), God calls out to Avraham, beckoning him
forth on a journey from his land, his birthplace, and his
parents' house to a land that God will show him. God's call is,
"*Lekh lekha.*" In Hebrew, "*lekh*" is the command "go!" Many
commentators throughout the generations have noted that
this would have been enough, simply saying "*lekh!*," "go!"
Yet the phrase is "*lekh lekha.*" In Hebrew "*lekha*" means "to you,"
or "for yourself." Avraham is asked to go forth not just physically, but spiritually as well. He is called to journey into the
unknown of the world and into the unknown parts of himself.
In so doing, God promises Avraham that he will become a
blessing to the world.

Ancient Jewish wisdom teaches that every one of us can
see ourselves as Avraham, continually called forth by *lekh lekha*.
The creative process is a vital tool for our journey. Working with
the unknown, seeing what emerges on our canvas or in our
notebook, helps us develop the capacity to navigate the unknown of our lives. By venturing into the unknown, we have
the opportunity to be surprised, to align with our truth, to
connect to the Divine, and to bring something new into the
world. As it was for Avraham, this call prompts us to venture
out into the world and, simultaneously, deep inside ourselves.
Engaging in the creative process is a practice of attuning our
system to be better able to hear that call when it comes, and to
have the courage to answer it when it does.

Materials needed

Small objects found in nature; tote bag; access to the outdoors.

Prompt

Venture on a brief excursion outside. This can be anywhere from the deep woods behind your home to a city street.
See if you can relax your eyes to look at the world around you through a soft gaze of wonder and enchantment. As you go, gather stones, leaves, petals, sticks, and other natural objects that you find on the ground. When you're done, find an open space and lay out what you've gathered. Create something with what you have, arranging the items you have found in a way that is pleasing to you. Offer gratitude for the gifts you've found. Notice in what ways (if any) this journey "out" brought you deeper "into" yourself.

Reflection

In this exercise you journeyed out into your neighborhood to harvest natural material and create something with what you found along the way.

- What did it feel like to venture out? What did you expect the experience to be like? How was it the same or different from your expectations?
- What was it like to go out with the intention to gather, not knowing what you'd find?
- How did you choose to work with what you found?
- In what ways (if any) did this "journey" connect you to yourself? To the Divine? To your creativity?
- How might the concept of journeying into the unknown support your own creative process?

The Place of All Possibility

ויאמר משה אל-אלהים הנה אנכי בא אל-בני ישראל ואמרתי להם אלהי
אבותיכם שלחני אליכם ואמרו-לי מה-שמו מה אמר אלהם:
ויאמר אלהים אל-משה **אהיה אשר אהיה** ויאמר כה תאמר לבני ישראל
אהיה שלחני אליכם.

Vayomer Moshe el Elohim hineh anokhi va el benei Yisrael ve'amarti lahem Elohei
avoteikhem shelachani aleikhem ve'amru li mah shemo mah omar aleihem:
*Vayomer Elohim el Moshe **Ehyeh Asher Ehyeh** vayomer koh tomar livnei Yisrael*
Ehyeh shelachani aleikhem.

MOSES SAID TO GOD, "WHEN I COME TO THE ISRAELITES AND SAY TO THEM,
'THE GOD OF YOUR FATHERS HAS SENT ME TO YOU,' AND THEY ASK ME,
'WHAT IS GOD'S NAME?' WHAT SHALL I SAY TO THEM?" AND GOD SPOKE TO MOSES,
"**I WILL BE THAT WHICH I WILL BE**." GOD SAID,
"THUS SHALL YOU SAY TO THE ISRAELITES, 'I WILL BE SENT ME TO YOU.'"
EXODUS 3:13–14

God Is Process

In Jewish thought, God is one but is called by many names in the sacred texts: mountain, guardian, rock, father, shield, compassion, presence, redeemer, womb, peace, king, and more. Each name is a refraction of one aspect of God's infinite being. Yet, in a moment of intimate exchange between God and Moses, one of God's most powerful and important names is revealed, one that seems to encompass all of the others. This name poetically epitomizes the creative process and sanctifies the process of becoming—the reality of eternal change that characterizes all life—and is a foundational pathway into the place of all possibility that we can follow in our own practice.

Aflame but not consumed

Let's set the scene. Moses, born to a Hebrew slave, raised as an Egyptian prince in Pharaoh's palace, lives unaware of his connection to the enslaved people constructing the pyramids at Pharaoh's behest. It is not until Moses observes the direct attack of an Egyptian taskmaster beating a slave that he is moved to intervene. In an attempt to protect the slaves, Moses strikes down the taskmaster, hiding his body in the sand to cover up his crime. It is here that we begin to see the ambivalence of Moses's allegiance: he is moved to protect the Hebrew people, and yet he also knows that to do so is to betray the culture and people he is a part of. Realizing that people will discover his offense, Moses prioritizes self-preservation and flees.[1] He settles in the land of Midian, marries a Midianite woman, and integrates into a new community of people. One day, as he is tending his father-in-law's flocks, he looks up and notices a "great sight": a bush that appears to be on fire, but is not consumed by the flames. Moses is compelled by this strange phenomenon. He asks, "Why doesn't the bush burn up?"[2] It is here, through the medium of the burning yet unscathed bush, that Moses hears the voice of God telling him that he, Moses, will lead the Hebrew people out of Egypt, from oppression to freedom.

Moses's story and the image of the burning bush offer many teachings for the creative process. We might say that the purpose of the creative process is to notice what burns in us and yet is not consumed. Anything that catches our attention and inflames us, in both inspiring and troubling ways, is fuel for our creative process, a voice from the universe calling us to pause, notice, and consider what wants to emerge or needs to be done. And through the story of Moses killing the Egyptian taskmaster, we also learn that realities we are unaware of, or that we suppress or deny, can erupt impulsively and uncontrollably; facing these realities and engaging with them can allow us to process them productively. The origin story of Moses reveals his complicated nature, and can help us understand why—as we'll see further on—the God of Process is revealed to him at this particular moment.

---

1   Exodus 2:14–15.
2   Exodus 3:3.

I will be that which I will be

In response to God's charge to Moses to liberate the Hebrew slaves from Egyptian bondage, Moses asks incredulously, "Who am I that I should go to Pharaoh, that I should bring the Children of Israel out of Egypt?" As he takes in the enormity of the task at hand, Moses's first response is to question his own fitness for the job (essentially asking, "Who am I to take on this task? Why me?"), but his question is also, in another sense, about his own identity—he is asking, truly, "Who am I?" In order to embrace his destiny, which is intimately tied to that of the Hebrew people, he must first know who he is. God, rather than answering Moses's question, instead assures him, replying, "Indeed, I will be with you." Moses, dissatisfied by this nonanswer and still anxious about his task, then tries a different approach. He asks, "When I go to the Israelites, and tell them that the God of their forefathers has sent me, they will say to me 'What is His name?' What shall I say to them?" In essence, he asks, "In this immense and risky undertaking of rebelling against Pharaoh and fleeing for freedom, how will I command authority in order to lead?" To this question God replies, "Tell them, 'I will be that which I will be [*Ehyeh Asher Ehyeh*]...sent me to you.'"[3]

How confusing and unsettling this must have been for Moses! At this pivotal moment, overwhelmed, nervous about the charge he's just been given, we can imagine Moses hoping for a less abstract answer. Doubting his own power and authority, and questioning his very identity, perhaps he was looking for a name of God that would command strength and reassurance, like "King," "Shield" or "Rock"—something that could communicate the confidence he himself lacked. Yet it is precisely in this moment that God identifies not as something formidable, and not even as a *thing* at all, but rather as a *process*—intangible, undefinable, and ever-changing.

---

3 Exodus 3:11–14.

This mysterious and intangible moniker may not have been what Moses *wanted* to hear, but it was what he *needed* to hear. God will reveal the unique face (or aspect) of God that each of us needs in the time that we need it, as if to say, "I will be what I will be … *when I will be it.*" In giving the name *Ehyeh Asher Ehyeh,* God is telling Moses that what is required in times like this — times that evoke existential fear, necessitate great risk-taking, and hold the potential for large-scale collective change — is not what we might expect. Rather than grasping towards a God that is predictable and sturdy, *Ehyeh Asher Ehyeh* teaches Moses that what he, and the people he is going to lead, actually need in that moment is a God of perpetual transformation.

The American Buddhist author Sandy Boucher writes that aspects of spirituality emerge in a culture "through people — individuals who recognize a particularly compelling expression of our humanity in practice, a divine figure, a belief, a system, and make it real in their lives."[4] God is everything, but it is the aspects and attributes of the Divine that we embody that determine how God shows up in the world. In this instance, Moses recognized, or was able to receive, the quality of God-as-Process. "We are all invited to become familiars with any manifestation of a divine force and to add what we learn to the rich story pool that animates human imagination," writes Pat B. Allen.[5] God can only manifest as what we imagine God to be, and what we bring into this world. Because humans are made *betzelem Elohim* (in the image of and in creative partnership with the Divine), what we call forth in God are the same qualities we call forth in ourselves. In identifying with the name *Ehyeh Asher Ehyeh,* God was telling Moses not only that *God* is to be known as this dynamic process of perpetual becoming, but that this name applies to Moses as well.

4 Sandy Boucher, *Discovering Kwan Yin, Buddhist Goddess of Compassion: A Path Toward Clarity and Peace* (Boston: Beacon Press, 2000), 5.

5 Pat B. Allen, *Art Is a Spiritual Path: Engaging the Sacred through the Practice of Art and Writing* (Boston: Shambhala Publications, 2005), 271.

When we hear God identifying as process, we can understand this to mean that we, too, can relish and embrace ourselves as *ehyeh asher ehyeh*: always changing, learning, and growing—ever-becoming who we are meant to be.

Who am I?

Having explored who God is in this moment, we can return to Moses's original question at the burning bush. Before asking who *God* is, Moses asks: "Who am I that I should go to Pharaoh?" *Who am I?* In Hebrew, "*Mi anokhi?*" There is a rhythmic, chant-like cadence to the Hebrew phrase, almost like an incantation. As the conversation between Moses and God moves on, and this question remains unanswered, for us readers, it continues to hang potently in the air. We feel the power of this question not only because we are aware of the complexity of Moses's upbringing and identity, but also because, within each of us, like Moses, multiple identities swirl. And like Moses, we may not be fully cognizant of the significance of these identities, the way they shape our beliefs, behaviors, and ideologies, or the subtle friction that might exist between them. Only by becoming conscious of the many threads of his identity can Moses access the *ehyeh* quality of his (and all) existence: mutability, malleability, fluidity, and flexibility.

Moses, like all of us, is a person of many identities, some of which are conflicting, ambiguous, or unknown to him. This complexity is encoded in Moses's name itself. After being weaned by his Hebrew mother Yocheved, he is named Moses by Pharaoh's daughter. Scholars debate whether this name is of Hebrew or Egyptian origins.[6] Midrash teaches that Moses in fact had ten different names, each reflecting a different

---

6   Ernest Klein, *Klein's Comprehensive Etymological Dictionary of the English Language*, rev. ed. (Amsterdam: Elsevier Publishing Company, 1971), 1006.

aspect of his life![7] He is a Hebrew man, born to a Hebrew
mother, yet raised by Pharaoh's daughter in the Egyptian palace.
Even while his first few years of life are spent in the royal
palace, he is brought back to his birth mother, Yocheved, to
nurse, shuttled back and forth between worlds. Moses is fed on
Pharaoh's food and his birth mother's milk; ingredients from
both cultures tangibly make up who he is.

Even Moses's question, "*Mi anokhi?*" is linguistically
complicated. Midrash teaches us that the word "*anokhi*"
is actually of Egyptian origin.[8] In the ensuing back and forth
with God, Moses says "I am not a man of words...I am a man
of heavy tongue."[9] We might understand this "heaviness of
tongue" as reflective of Moses's difficulty expressing himself
as he moves between identities and languages. The challenge
of navigating intersecting and sometimes contradictory
identities with confidence and clarity is something that's
familiar to many of us.

Moses's Egyptian lineage is that of royalty; his Hebrew
lineage is that of slavery. It's no wonder he asks this essential
question. Moses comes from both privilege and oppression;
he is of both cultures and neither. We can hear in his question
both a straightforward question ("Who am I?"), as well as an
attempt at evading the responsibility being appointed to him
("Who am I to take on this task?"). In this question, we can also
hear Moses groping towards an understanding of his unique,
complex, and contradictory make-up, which will allow him to
more deeply appreciate why he, of all people, might be perfectly suited for actualizing this seemingly impossible task of
leading his people to liberation.

Each one of us is made up of multiple cultures and
identities. Like Moses, some parts we accept and embrace,
while others we deny or don't even know about. If we can feel

---

7   Vayikra Rabbah 1:3.
8   Midrash Tanchuma (Buber), Yitro 16.
9   Exodus 4:10.

empathy and compassion for Moses in this difficult work of integrating the complexity of his identity, perhaps we can feel that same compassion for ourselves in this regard. The process of bringing these various aspects of our lives into consciousness is multilayered: it has emotional, practical, and psychological aspects; it might be painful and lonely; and it can, at times, cause us to challenge closely held narratives about ourselves or our most important relationships. This work of sorting through our lineages, and untangling the threads of stories we've inherited, takes time. The creative process offers us unique tools for doing this work. Supported by the pleasure of art-making, our mind and heart become able to open, soften, and trust that the information and knowledge we need to glean will show itself as we are able to bear it.

I will be with you

When we take one small step into this challenging and sacred endeavor of emergence, growth, and becoming—when we turn towards the work of our lives—we can feel God turning towards us. Through moments of synchronicity, release of energy, instructive dreams, a renewed lightness of being, or the excitement that comes through setting off on a new journey, we can feel that God is with us. We become enlivened and inspired to continue on this path.

In response to Moses's question *"Mi anokhi?"* God answers *"Ehyeh imakh"*—"I will be with you."[10] It's no accident that the language God uses to answer both of Moses's questions (*Who am I?* and *Who are You?*) is similar; the two statements are linked together through a poetic repetition of the phrase *"ehyeh,"* meaning "I will be." Essentially, it is as if God is telling Moses: "I will be that which I will be, you will become that which you will become, and it is through this process of

---

10 Exodus 3:12.

growth and change that you will know that you and I are forever connected." In his explanation of this verse, the thirteenth-century commentator Ramban writes, "And what is the meaning of I Will Be That Which I Will Be? As you are with Me, so I am with you. If you open your hands to the needy, so will I open my hands."[11] On one hand, we might hear this interpretation as conditional, that it is only if we support those in need that God will choose to do so as well. But we might also hear this as relational: to the extent that we are able to open our aperture to let God in, God is able to open and flow to us and through us, into the world. For in fact, we are God's hands in the studio of life.

In the Torah, the Israelites' relationship to the Divine is understood through the language of "covenant," an agreement in which God and the people commit, and are bound, to one another. Today, we can imagine that each one of us is invited into our own version of a covenantal relationship with the Divine. To enter into this relationship is to accept, embrace, and partner with the Source of All Life in the process of cocreating the world. We might ask: How do we maintain a partnership with a force that is ever-changing? Inherently, our relationship must be dynamic. It is a commitment that is not only always in process—it is in fact a commitment to *be* in process. This is our *avodah*, our spiritual work: a partnership of coevolution and creative unfolding. We commit to not pinning down God— or ourselves—to being any one thing. Through this partnership, we assert that God is not something static that can be encountered once and understood forever based on that one encounter. Rather, God is dynamic, changing, and evolving alongside us. And we, human beings made *betzelem Elohim*, in the divine image, are likewise not static creations, but rather are in our own process of always becoming. God is process, and we and God, together with the rest of creation, are in the process of birthing and rebirthing the reality in which we live.

---

11 Ramban on Exodus 3:13 (quoting Sefer veHizhir. See Torah Sheleimah, paragraph 188).

A catalyst for creative unfolding

It's no accident that the name *Ehyeh Asher Ehyeh* is given in the same breath that God calls upon Moses to lead the people from the oppression of Egypt to liberation. *Mitzrayim*, the name for Egypt in Hebrew, contains the Hebrew word *tzar*, meaning a "narrow strait." The Psalmist sings, "*Min hameitzar karati ya, anani bamerchav ya*": "From the narrow strait I called out to the Divine, I was answered in divine expansiveness."[12] What are the "narrow straits" we face today? This psalm prompts us to cry out against (and from within) those things that cause our minds and hearts to become narrow and constricted. What would a world without poverty, war, or oppression look like? It seems as unimaginable now as it did to the Israelites living under Pharaoh's brutal regime back then. And yet, in partnership with *Ehyeh Asher Ehyeh*, Moses and the Israelites leave the narrow straits of *Mitzrayim* and enter into the wide-open expanse, the *merchav* of the wilderness, on the other side.

To move from narrowness to expansiveness, from a culture of coercion to one of connection and care, from a society based on exploitation to one of mutual thriving, we can call upon *Ehyeh Asher Ehyeh*, the God who is always becoming. We can partner with, sing to, pray for, be guided, supported, and infused by that force that says that the way things are is not the only way things can be. God is the catalyst for creative unfolding into the place of all possibility. There is so much more possible in our world beyond what we have created thus far. In times of struggle and fear, we can reach towards God as possibility and creativity, as that which opens us to the limitless power of our own radical imagination to create beyond the confines of what *has been*, guiding us towards the future of what yet *could be*.

12 Psalms 118:5.

The ongoing aliveness of the world

Ehyeh Asher Ehyeh speaks not only to the ways in which we engage *in* creative process—but also to the understanding that we, ourselves, *are* a creative process! We need only look to contemporary science to see that this is not only metaphorically, but quite literally, true. There is nothing static about us. Scientists estimate that, every day, roughly 300 billion of our cells are replaced, the equivalent of about 1 percent of all our bodies' cells. Over two to three months, this is the equivalent of an entirely new "you."[13] Rather than a human *being*, we might more accurately say we are a human *becoming*. We are constituted by millions of beings that make up who we are. As recent data shows, only 50 percent of the cells in our bodies are human; the rest are microbes—including bacteria, yeasts, viruses, and even insects.[14] Together, these make up what is known as our microbiome. Lest we dismiss these creatures as unimportant, recent research has found that our microbiome is so critical to our existence that, rather than viewing a human being as an individual entity, many scientists consider us to be *symbiotic organisms,* beings defined by a particular set of relationships: there is the host (us), all the other organisms that live upon and within us, and the ecological landscapes in which we live.[15] *"Mi anokhi?"* Who *are* we? Indeed. We are the ongoing aliveness of the world. We are the meeting point of trillions of cells, yeasts, fungi, and more that come together to constitute us. We are constantly sloughing, shifting, shedding, growing, changing, as every being that makes up our body goes through its own process of becoming. We are interdependent with, and interpenetrated by, millions of other beings in the ongoing

13 Mark Fischetti and Jen Christiansen, "A New You in 80 Days," *Scientific American*, April 2021, 76.

14 Ron Sender, Shai Fuchs, and Ron Milo, "Revised Estimates for the Number of Human and Bacteria Cells in the Body," PLOS *Biology* 14, no. 8 (2016).

15 Amy Loughman and Tarsh Bates, "Microbes Aren't the Enemy, They Are a Big Part of Who We Are," *The Conversation*, July 3, 2017.

cocreation of our life, which is never separate from the dynamic process that continuously creates and recreates the world.

There is something at once terrifying and electrifying in the realization that we are not only *in process*—we *are process*. This cocreative process on which our lives depend can never be completely controlled, nor should it be. How could we possibly supervise millions of organisms to do the work necessary to balance and bring us into life? There is a beauty and a relief in surrendering to life as it moves through and within us. And there is a comfort to be found in knowing that we are not alone. "The idea of being cut off from the other," writes German biologist, philosopher, and writer Andreas Weber, "is perhaps the fundamental error of our civilization."[16] Such an alienated perspective engenders a sense of isolation and disconnection that causes our souls to wither and recoil from what we perceive as a hostile world. Yet, in reality, we are never cut off, never alone. Not only do the stories, songs, and dreams of our ancestors exist within us, but so too do the cells of stardust, volcano ash, and prehistoric trees. Remnants of all that has ever been are woven into the fabric of who we are and who we will become.

The awe and wonder of creative becoming

As a foundational pathway to the place of all possibility, *Ehyeh Asher Ehyeh* invites us into the sacredness inherent in the ongoing process of becoming. God is ever-changing, and so are we. In the creative process, everything is always in motion—the position of the clouds as we try to photograph a landscape, the way our page looks after the next color has been added. Such constant change can evoke fear and trepidation, as something we've come to know subtly (or not so subtly)

---

16 Dr. Andreas Weber, *Matter and Desire: An Erotic Ecology* (White River Junction, VT: Chelsea Green Publishing, 2017), 26.

shifts (e.g., ourselves, a partner, a situation in our community). To engage in the creative process as a practice of inquiry and exploration is to develop openness and resilience to change. We work with what we have on hand to transform it into something else: dabs of paint become an image, a block of clay gives way to a sculpture, the vibrations of guitar strings become a song.

Yet, creative process is not only about what is created externally—at a deeper level, creative process is about what is created within each of us. The act of creating puts internal and spiritual work into motion. Every time we engage in the creative process, we are nourishing the part of ourselves that believes that change is possible. We are carving the neural pathways of our imagination that let us open to ideas, images, and visions beyond what we currently see. *Ehyeh Asher Ehyeh* proclaims that we have a role to play in the vital, sacred work of transformation.

ויאמר משה אל-אלהים הנה אנכי בא אל-בני ישראל ואמרתי להם אלהי
אבותיכם שלחני אליכם ואמרו-לי מה-שמו מה אמר אלהם:
ויאמר אלהים אל-משה **אהיה אשר אהיה** ויאמר כה תאמר לבני ישראל אהיה
שלחני אליכם.

*Vayomer Moshe el Elohim hineh anokhi va el benei Yisrael ve'amarti lahem Elohei
avoteikhem shelachani aleikhem ve'amru li mah shemo mah omar aleihem:
Vayomer Elohim el Moshe **Ehyeh Asher Ehyeh** vayomer koh tomar livnei Yisrael Ehyeh
shelachani aleikhem.*

MOSES SAID TO GOD, "WHEN I COME TO THE ISRAELITES AND SAY TO THEM,
'THE GOD OF YOUR FATHERS HAS SENT ME TO YOU,' AND THEY ASK ME,
'WHAT IS GOD'S NAME?' WHAT SHALL I SAY TO THEM?" AND GOD SPOKE TO MOSES,
"I WILL BE THAT WHICH I WILL BE." GOD SAID,
"THUS SHALL YOU SAY TO THE ISRAELITES, 'I WILL BE SENT ME TO YOU.'"
EXODUS 3:13–14

God Is Process   EHYEH ASHER EHYEH   אהיה אשר אהיה

In Jewish sacred texts, God is called by many names including:
Rock, Guardian, Womb, King, Lord, Shield—yet all are limited
approximations of God's infinite being. The Torah describes an
intimate exchange between God and Moses. Here, Moses asks
God how he should identify God to the people (Exodus 3:14).
In this one-on-one conversation next to the burning bush, Moses
asks God: "When I come to the Israelites and say that You
sent me, what should I tell them Your name is?" God answers:
"Ehyeh Asher Ehyeh" ("I shall be that which I shall be"). In this
instance, God identifies not as person, not as place, but as
process. We, too, as Moses learns, are in process, and together
with God, we transform that which is into that which will be.

Materials needed

Any supplies that you have easily on hand that feel exciting to work with. This can be as simple as a ballpoint pen and scrap paper, bare feet on the earth, a pile of sticks and leaves in your front yard, or your own voice.

Prompt

Let this exercise be a way to let the material we've been exploring unfold within you. Pick up any material that intrigues you, and simply begin. When creating, we often tend to overthink what we're doing. We want to map out the process and know exactly what the end result will be. Instead, try the reverse. Allow each brushstroke, each note, each move, to lead to the next, rather than predetermining a plan. Use this as a time to follow sensation: How does each action feel, sound, lead you to the next? Be with what is and let that be the inspiration for what will be next. Follow what has energy for you in each moment.

Reflection

In this exercise, you followed your intuition and imagination to create without a preconceived idea of what you would make.

↝   How did you begin?

↝   What was it like to follow sensation? Where did you
      notice it in your body?

↝   Did anything new about *Ehyeh Asher Ehyeh* come to mind
      as you created?

The Place of All Possibility

בן בג בג אומר: **הפך בה והפך בה**, דכלא בה.

Ben Bag Bag omer: *hafokh bah vahafokh bah, dekhula vah.*

BEN BAG BAG SAYS: **TURN IT AND TURN IT**, FOR EVERYTHING IS IN IT.
PIRKEI AVOT 5:22

What Else Could This Be?

How do we responsively relate to the world, to each other, to ourselves, if everything is in a process of constant change? The rabbis of the Mishnah offer one answer. In Pirkei Avot, a collection of ethical teachings and maxims, we find the following teaching, given in the name of Ben Bag Bag, a learned scholar of the first generation of rabbinic sages (around 20–40 CE): "*Hafokh bah vahafokh bah, dekhula vah.*" "Turn it and turn it, for everything is in it."[1] As a pathway to the place of all possibility, *hafokh bah* calls us to acknowledge, seek out, and engage the multiple truths contained within any one verse, story, image, person, experience, or idea.

Turn it and turn it

In this teaching, Ben Bag Bag is proposing an orientation to sacred text; "it" is the Torah. For the ancient rabbis, as for many Jews today, Torah—the lessons, laws, and insight it offers—is central and essential to their lives. Torah is viewed not only as precious and in need of protection, but also as enlivened through inquiry, learning, and discussion. Torah is experienced as a wellspring of life, a repository of wisdom, and a source of blessing. At the same time, throughout the

---

1   Pirkei Avot 5:22.

generations it has also been incredibly complicated, often contradictory, and confusingly ambiguous to decipher what any passage, verse, or word of Torah even means!

One reaction to something confusing or complex is to try to simplify it. In this vein, rather than "turn it and turn it," the instruction might have been: "turn it…over to someone else who will tell you what it means." Or: "turn…away from it, and let someone else deal with it." In other words, let someone you consider smarter, more learned, or more authoritative interpret the text for you. This approach might make the text easier to understand, but it also risks homogenizing it by foreclosing the diverse meanings that can arise if we each approach the Torah from our own perspective. Our own curiosity and agency as readers are lost in this outsourced approach. But Pirkei Avot encourages just the opposite: *Turn it and turn it.* We should all engage Torah (and the world!) in such a hands-on and sustained way to find ever-new facets within it—and within ourselves.

Everything is in it

Taken in context, "turn it and turn it" is an instruction for how to approach Torah. Yet, the wisdom of these words reaches far beyond the *beit midrash*. "Turn it and turn it" can provide us with a framework for how to live as agents of creativity and trans-formation in a complex and ever-changing world. We might ask: What in our own lives is laden with meaning, complicated, and at times confusing? What do we turn away from, rather than towards? What have we cut ourselves off from, out of frustration or discomfort, rather than seeking to understand the source of these reactions? What in our lives is worthy of more attention, rather than avoidance?

"Turn it and turn it, for *everything* is in it": the good, the bad, the beautiful, the ugly, the harsh, the merciful, and more. Within Torah there are no simple characters—not even the most revered heroes like Avraham and Moses are paragons of virtue at all times. There are stories that depict deception, betrayal, conquest, and destruction; others that highlight love, friendship, bravery, and beauty. The way Torah opens within us when we engage it is compared to the way a rose's petals open outward as it blooms.[2] Torah is not only the ambrosial scent of the rose, its velvety petals, alluring colors, and elegant shape— it is also its sturdy stem and sharp thorns. Yet, just because something is prickly doesn't mean we should necessarily keep our distance. Like the harsh stories in Torah with the potential to wound, the thorns on a rose serve to protect the plant, causing us to approach it with care and consideration. For the rose, thorns cause species that come to feed on the plant, like caterpillars, to move much slower in their consumption process. In fact, research has shown that "the spines [on a plant stem] not only slowed the caterpillars but also interfered with their footing and forced them into more acrobatic maneuvers."[3] Caterpillars actually coevolved with rose bushes; the thorns on the plant forced the caterpillar to develop increased dexterity and flexibility. Torah study offers us a similar opportunity. The more we stay in relationship with both the prickles and the promise of these ancient words, the more capable and coordinated we become, and the more our minds, hearts, and souls are able to navigate difficulty to discover wisdom.

This is a practice that we can return to over time, engaging Torah again and again—turning and turning it—throughout our lives. Like the caterpillar and the rose bush, our relationship with Torah can be a coevolution that depends on us maintaining an ongoing relationship. And the practice of sorting through the stories of Torah cultivates within us the capacity and the discipline to sift through and thoughtfully engage the many stories that make us who we are—those we've created,

2 See Ellen Frankel and Betsy Platkin Teutsch, *The Encyclopedia of Jewish Symbols* (Lanham, MD: Jason Aronson, Inc., 1995), 139.
3 Christie Wilcox, "The Thorny Truth About Spine Evolution," *Quanta Magazine*, June 14, 2017.

those we've received, and those we unearth over the course of
a lifetime. The more we stay in relationship to Torah, the more
agile we become at finding the layers of sweetness and generativity contained therein, and the more adept we become at
creatively navigating the many layers of our lives.

Turn in it

The phrase *hafokh bah* can mean "turn it," as we have discussed,
but it can also be translated as "turn *in* it." While this is only
a slight grammatical variation, it opens up a more intimate,
experiential understanding of this idea. When we turn something, we remain stationary, holding the thing that we're
turning at arm's length. To turn *in* something is to enter into
the thing itself—to allow ourselves to be moved and affected
by it in a visceral way. Think of a closely held idea, something
you strongly believe in and hold dear. To *turn* it is to surface
different perspectives of this idea, including those you don't
believe in. To turn *in* the idea is to actually try on these perspectives, and through your imagination, allow yourself to
inhabit these stances. Rather than intellectually considering
this idea from afar, to turn *in* it is to notice what this idea
arouses in you—what emotions come up, what new insights
arise, how your feelings towards the idea (or those who hold
this belief) shift and change. To turn *in* it is to allow ourselves
to become porous to a particular perspective and all it evokes,
even if only temporarily.

These two interpretations—"turn it" and "turn *in* it"—
become tangible when explored through the creative process.
Imagine a drawing on the table in front of you that you
have been working on. Following the invitation of *hafokh bah*,
you might turn the page in a different direction, changing
its orientation to you. What was right side up is now upside
down. What looked, perhaps, like the outline of a human
face now appears like a landscape. Both images are there,

both possibilities exist, and more. By turning the page, you have generated more possibilities for what your creation could be. Not only that, you have loosened up your assumptions, making your mind more supple and open.

To turn *in* the drawing is to imagine that whatever has appeared on the page is a world in and of itself that has its own logic, and to inhabit that world, even if for a brief time. Rather than generating endless possibilities of what the lines on the page could be, we commit ourselves to one vision and spend our energy bringing it more fully into being. For example, a circle that looks like an open mouth: we might be compelled to add teeth, tongue, and lips, even if we have no idea who or what this creature is or where the image might go from here. We immerse ourselves in the process, letting ourselves notice and be moved to action by the clues that show up in the image itself, regardless of how they may or may not make sense to our rational mind.

By allowing new angles and interpretations to emerge, the process of *turning it* can help us better appreciate the permutational breadth of a given story, idea, or image. On the other hand, the practice of *turning in it* allows us to more fully inhabit a story, idea, or image's particular depths. The two can complement one another, deepening our emotional, intellectual, and somatic understanding of whatever is before us. Each approach is useful towards different ends and is generative in different ways.

We can gain insight into the world by going into ourselves, and we can gain insight into ourselves by reflecting on our lived experience in the world. These two vantage points merge with and emerge from one another. Our creative process is nourished when we oscillate back and forth between the two, allowing our lived experience to inform our self-reflection and our self-reflection to ground and guide our actions in the world. Though we separate "self" and "world" in order to better understand each, in fact, they are one and the same. While we often speak about "the world" as if it is something "out there," distinct from "us," Jewish tradition teaches *adam olam katan, olam adam gadol:* the human being is a microcosm of the world, the world is a macrocosm of the human being.[4] We are not only *of* the earth—we are each a tiny world in and of ourselves, reflecting and effecting the broader whole. That which we wish to see in the world we must find within ourselves; and those attributes and values we cultivate within ourselves are not only for us, but for the world.

Turning towards

Both aspects of *hafokh bah* can support us at difficult moments in our personal and professional lives. Personally, I'm thinking here about the sudden, tragic death of a dear student and community member whom I had mentored and worked with for a number of years. On one hand, I needed to *turn and turn* my understanding of this person and of myself—our relationship, experiences we'd had together, expectations I'd held— seeing it all from different perspectives. This process of intellectual reflection uncovered feelings that I had been previously unaware of. On the other hand, I then needed to take those feelings and *turn in them* to fully unpack what was there. To do so, I turned to the creative process, offering a session to many people touched by this loss, in which I also engaged.

As a rabbi, I am often holding the space for others to access and articulate genuine emotion. In this case, the session was for everyone in our community who was navigating grief in the wake of this loss. Yet my own feelings in this moment were as raw and intense as anyone's. Having the added support of the creative process gave me a way not only to serve others, opening a space for them to explore and share their feelings, but also gave me the means to process the intense and complicated emotions this death brought up for me.

4   Midrash Tanchuma (Buber), Pekudei 3:3.

You don't have to be a clergy person to know this need. As caregivers in whatever capacity — therapist, teacher, parent, medical professional, adult child with ailing parents — there is so much that each of us is holding. Many of us in these positions are well-acquainted with the first aspect of *hafokh bah* — turning things over intellectually — but have had less opportunity, support, or time to explore our own emotional experience through the second aspect — the complex emotional exploration of *turning in it.* But we, too, are entitled to the care and support that we offer to others. In fact, without this, we can become impaired and can lose our connection to those we wish to serve and uplift. *Hafokh bah* points us to the creative process as a point of care for ourselves. Rather than being denied or foreclosed, our feelings are given space, containment, and respect, thereby offering us not only relief in the moment, but a sense of reconnection to ourselves and to those we care for.

Like a prayer

There is an aspect of turning something over and over that is akin to prayer. One of the first instances of prayer in the Torah is found in Genesis. Isaac and Rebecca are struggling to conceive a child, and Isaac turns to God, asking for God to open Rebecca's womb. The word that is used for Isaac's beseeching of God is "*vaye'ater.*" This word comes from the root *ayin-tav-resh,* whose primary constellation of meanings is to pray or supplicate, but which the sages connect to a less common meaning, a "pitchfork."[5] A passage in the Talmud teaches:

> "*Rabbi Yitzchak said: Why are the prayers of the righteous compared to a pitchfork [eter], as in the verse: 'And God let Himself be entreated [vaye'ater]'? This indicates that just*

---

5   Babylonian Talmud, Sukkah 14a.

as this pitchfork turns over grain from one place to another, so the
prayer of the righteous turns over the attributes of the Holy One,
Blessed be, from the attribute of anger to the attribute of mercy."[6]

In agriculture, pitchforks are used to prepare the ground for
planting by loosening, lifting, and turning over the soil.
The top layers of dirt, once hardened and dried out, are mixed
around and aerated; new life is breathed into the soil. Bugs
scamper about, worms wriggle through. The ground soil is now
ready for sowing. We might imagine Isaac's prayer similarly,
like a pitchfork, stirring up energy within himself, and within
God, opening up the space for something generative to occur.

Just as prayer stirs energy, and a pitchfork mixes soil,
when we turn and turn our vantage point on something, we
bring up rich layers that were not readily visible, loosening
what has become hard-packed so that life can blossom anew.
In turning our understanding of something over again and
again, we give ourselves a chance to move from a place of judgment, fear, or pain, to one of mercy, compassion, and flexibility.
Instead of taking impulsive action towards a goal conceived
in the heat of the moment, we aerate our reality to let things
soften and relax so that other feelings and thoughts have an
opportunity to come to the surface. To turn it and turn it in
this way creates the conditions, time, and space needed for
movement, generativity, and transformation.

Turn it on its head

The act of turning is sacred. In the phrase *hafokh bah*, we find
etymological resonance with two of the most sacred days in
the Jewish calendar: Purim and Yom Kippur. Counterintuitively,
Jewish teachings suggest that Purim, a day of feasting and
great merriment, is spiritually equivalent to Yom Kippur,

6   Babylonian Talmud, Yevamot 64a.

a day of strict fasting and atonement, and that both of these
days, despite their polar opposite orientations, are considered
to be the holiest times of the year. In fact, it is taught that in
the World to Come (that is, the world in its most perfect, holy
state), the Jewish holidays that are celebrated today will no
longer exist—except for Purim and Yom Kippur.[7] While Yom
Kippur is commonly recognized as the holiest day of the year
for Jews, the inclusion of Purim here is unexpected. Purim is
a carnivalesque holiday. In addition to reading the story of
Purim from the Scroll of Esther, it is celebrated by dressing up
in costumes, creating Purim spiels (satirical and silly plays
that poke fun at the things we normally treat with seriousness,
including politics, authority figures, and even ourselves),
giving gifts, and gathering to eat, drink, and party.

So what imbues Purim with such holiness? The story
and customs of Purim are rooted in precisely this principle
of *hafokh bah*—of reversal and turning around. Essentially, the
holiday is all about allowing ourselves to flip, invert, and
otherwise shake up all that we think we know. At the center
of the Purim story is Queen Esther, the beauty queen with
seemingly no political capital who becomes the most powerful
person in the land and is able to reverse a genocidal decree
against her people. Roles and dynamics are upended; fates are
overturned. The Purim story can be encapsulated by the
phrase found in the text, *"venafokhu,"* "and it was reversed."[8]
And, of course, *venafokhu* is a variation on the same root as *hafokh*.

On Purim, we are encouraged to shake things up, turn
them around, and see the world, and ourselves, from a new
angle. To do so, Jewish tradition teaches that we are to loosen
our minds *"ad delo yada,"* until we enter into a state of not
knowing.[9] Throughout the day's festivities we hold lightly who
we've been and what we usually believe, and enter into the

---

7 Midrash Mishlei 9:1.

8 Megillat Esther 9:1.

9 Babylonian Talmud, Megillah 7b:7.

sometimes silly, yet seriously sacred task of turning our world and our perception upside down.

The name *Purim* comes from the drawing of lots (it is the plural form of the Hebrew word "*pur*," meaning "lot," as in "lottery") that the king's trusted advisor, Haman, cast to determine when he would carry out his plot to annihilate the Jewish people. But Jewish wisdom offers a deeper spiritual meaning in the name of this holiday, drawn from the similar sounds found in the words *Pur*-im and Kip-*pur* (as in Yom Kippur). Although there is no etymological connection between these two names, the rabbis riffed on the auditory resonance: Yom Kippur, when we seek atonement from one another and from God through a strict fast and full day of intensive prayer, and which is regarded by many as the most sacred day in the Jewish calendar, is (the rabbis tell us) *"yom kePurim." "Yom"* means "day," and the prefix *"ke"* means "like," so Yom Kippur becomes "a day like Purim."[10] The nineteenth-century rabbi Israel Friedman of Ruzhyn, known as the Rebbe of Ruzhyn, took this idea even further, saying, "The smaller is 'hanging onto' the bigger,"[11] meaning Purim — not Yom Kippur! — is in fact the holiest day of the year.

At first glance, it may seem odd to connect these two holidays. On Purim, we indulge in celebratory food and drink, dress in colorful costumes, and entertain ourselves with frivolity and festivity, while on Yom Kippur, we abstain from food and drink, solemnly take accountability for our misdeeds, and seek forgiveness from those we've harmed. Rather than regarding the wild, creative, carnivalesque Purim simply as a day of debauchery (as many do), the sages saw this holiday's flipping, turning, and reversing of ideas and identities as intimately, even if paradoxically, connected to the deep, spiritual, soul-work of Yom Kippur. In preparation for the

---

10 Zohar 57b.

11 See David Ingber, "Empty and Full: Pomegranates, Bells and the Dual Mind of the Holy," Sefaria, accessed February 8, 2024.

Day of Atonement, we identify and sit with the times in which we've missed the mark over the prior year, turning these instances over and over, seeing our actions from the perspective of others involved, allowing ourselves to face the effects our actions have had, on others as well as ourselves. Through different rituals and energies, both Purim and Yom Kippur invite us to dig into, and turn over, how we see ourselves, how we understand our actions, and how we relate to each other. Whether in the rainbow colors of Purim or the starkness of Yom Kippur, these two topsy-turvy days in the Jewish calendar invite us into *hafokh bah* — to turn it and turn it, again and again, until healing, release, atonement, forgiveness, and freedom are found.

Upside down and right side up

When pondering the teaching of *hafokh bah*, one might ask, is its meaning to turn it once, so that it's inverted, and then turn it again, so it goes back to how it was before? Or is its meaning to turn it and turn it — and keep turning it, ad infinitum?[12] While the latter interpretation is the traditional understanding, the former is also powerful in its own way. That is, to take an idea or belief and turn it entirely upside down, for the sake of play or exploration. Even if afterwards you end up returning to your original perspective, you can often reveal new dimensions of whatever it is you are turning around, and of yourself in relation to it. For example, after I learned the rabbinic interpretation about the link between Purim and Yom Kippur, I never experienced either of them the same. Though I returned to the customary observances of each holiday, there is now a glimmer of joy and festivity on Yom Kippur, and a mystical depth to Purim that was not there before.

---

12 I'm grateful to Lex Rolfberg for his comment on this during his 2022 interview with me on *Judaism Unbound's* "Torah of Creativity" episode.

To invert reality is not only holy; it is healthy. "In order
to break limiting patterns, it is often necessary to take a dis-
tinctly different posture, or stance, such as turning ourselves
upside down to get another view of a restrictive pattern or
stuck place in consciousness that is being experienced" writes
Angeles Arrien in *The Tarot Handbook*.[13] We can experience the
physical benefits of this in our bodies. If you've ever practiced
yoga, you know the power of inversions. To invert is to bring
the head below the heart. Our thinking mind comes closer to
the earth and our feeling heart is raised up towards the sky.
These poses are some of the most challenging for yoga practi-
tioners to master, but they are said to have many physiological
benefits: increased blood circulation, lymphatic drainage, and
spinal strengthening, to name a few.[14] Physical inversions offer
an embodied metaphor of the wisdom of reversals: in them,
our typical way of existing, and our point of view, is literally
turned upside down as our body is realigned and re-enlivened.

What else could this be?

The principle of *hafokh bah* ultimately leads us back to the
polyvocality and multiplicity of the Torah. As we've discussed
in previous chapters, traditional rabbinic commentary is
dense with multiple perspectives; diverse and even contradictory viewpoints are not only present, but often deeply valued.
In fact, the ability to see other sides of an issue was considered
so essential in ancient times that, in order to serve on the
Sanhedrin (the Jewish High Court), one had to prove their
adeptness in this regard. The Talmud relates, "Rav Yehuda said
that Rav said: We place on the Sanhedrin only one who knows
how to purify a *sheretz* [an impure creepy crawly thing] using

13 Angeles Arrien, *The Tarot Handbook: Practical Applications of Ancient Visual Symbols*, 2nd
ed. (Sonoma, CA: Arcus Publishing Company 1994), 69.
14 "Yoga Inversion: A Guide to What It Is, and How You Can Benefit," *Healthline*,
February 17, 2021.

Torah."[15] That is, no one may be seated as a member of the court until they show that they can prove the purity of an animal Torah has specifically designated as impure through the logic and laws laid out in the Torah itself. To be seen as able to adjudicate the community's most important legal issues, a person must demonstrate their capacity to take a seemingly black-and-white issue (such as the kosher status of an animal) and show the entire color spectrum within it.

The pathway of *hafokh bah*—this ability to turn things around, and show them from another perspective—is foundational to the creative process as well. How many different angles can we understand something from? Can we find the joy as well as the somberness, the depth and the levity in this process? Through continuously asking, "What else could this be?"—of ourselves, of others, of our creations, and of the complex and challenging situations we encounter in our personal and communal life—we cultivate an appreciation for multiplicity, and the ability to hold multiple truths and perspectives at once. Can we allow ourselves to bring the unfettered freedom of the creative process to Torah and to our own identities the way we might allow ourselves to play with paint on the canvas, or words in a poem? To try this here, or try that there? *Hafokh bah* invites us to continually be in a state of curiosity and to ask the sacred, sometimes scary, more-often-than-not soul-rejuvenating question: *What else could this (or I) be?*

The principle of *hafokh bah* is inherent in the creative process. Not only do we turn and turn our materials to open new vantage points, but through the practice of art-making, we allow the feelings that exist within us to shift and evolve as we create, turning *us* in the process. The creative process utilizes whatever materials we have at our disposal to keep our hands busy so that challenging ideas and emotions have a chance to burn, churn, and turn into something else—clarity, new conceptions, or compassionate action. On any given day,

---

15 Babylonian Talmud, Sanhedrin 17a.

we may start out feeling angry, confused, lethargic, or sad. Through the creative process we open ourselves up so that we have a chance to inquire into and allow those emotions to shift. Just as Isaac's prayer turned over the attributes of God from anger to compassion, when we create, we turn over *our* emotions. To create is to transform not only the external material we work with, but the internal material of who we are.

בן בג בג אומר: **הפך בה והפך בה**, דכלא בה.

*Ben Bag Bag omer: **hafokh bah vahafokh bah**, dekhula vah.*

BEN BAG BAG SAYS: **TURN IT AND TURN IT,** FOR EVERYTHING IS IN IT.
PIRKEI AVOT 5:22

Turn It and Turn It   HAFOKH BAH   הפך בה

"Turn it and turn it, for everything is in it" (Pirkei Avot 5:22). Written with regards to our relationship to Torah, this verse from the Mishnah teaches that we are meant to be continually shifting our vantage point, seeing things from new angles, and allowing our perspective to change. What if we saw Torah as more than just the text on the page, but also as the text of our lives? This instruction to "turn it and turn it" can be broadened as an invitation for how we might approach people we interact with, media we consume, and even how we see ourselves. Just as Torah is complex and many-layered, so too do each of us contain multitudes. How might your life, work, identity, and relationships change if you continuously "turn" what is before you to view it from a new perspective?

Materials needed

A sheet of paper; any kind of drawing, sketching, or painting supplies; a timer set for ten minutes.

Prompt

Brainstorm five ways you might "turn" or otherwise change your relationship to the piece of paper in front of you. Then, with the timer set for ten minutes, begin by making marks on the page in any way that is pleasing to you. Over the course of the ten minutes, "turn" your relationship to the piece of paper in at least three different ways.

If you need some help with ideas for ways to "turn it":

↝   Rotate the piece of paper.
↝   Close your eyes while creating.
↝   Flip the piece of paper over.
↝   Change the angle of your body in relationship to the paper.
↝   Fold the paper and work on it as it is folded into a
      different shape.

Reflection

In this exercise you physically changed your perspective on what was before you.

↝   What was it like to have to turn the page? Were you
      surprised? Relieved? Curious? Frustrated? What did you
      discover?
↝   Who or what in your life would you like to be able to see
      from a new perspective?

The Place of All Possibility

Conclusion

We live in times of unprecedented challenge and change.
From the political to the personal, it often feels like we're hitting
a wall. Stuck in cycles of anxiety and exploitation, we face a
crisis of imagination. We need new pathways to possibility.
As a species and as a society we've successfully cultivated our
capacity for certainty and control, for separation and subjugation.
Now, for our own sanity and the planet's survival, we need to
cultivate our capacity for uncertainty, for openness, for connection to each other and all that unites us. We need to reclaim
our inherent creativity as the seat of our deepest power.

Throughout this book, I've shared some of what I've
learned as an educator and spiritual leader in my personal and
professional journeys to what I call "the place of all possibility":
the expansive, nourishing, and profound realm that is opened
up by the creative process. In my work facilitating and training
leaders in the Jewish Studio Process, I continue to discover
the transformative potential of this unique blend of creative
practice and ancient Jewish wisdom. This synergy of Torah and
creativity unlocks much-needed new possibility and imagination
when applied to challenges as diverse as processing grief,
professional burnout, societal injustice, and so much more.

Ancient Jewish wisdom offers profound insights and a
creative toolbox that can and should be accessible to all people.
These particular traditions and texts are especially potent
when applied to the times we live in. I invite you to find what

resonates for you in Torah and bring it into your creative process
and into your life. Creativity is the root of our human nature.
The story is still being written.

* *
*

After each day of creation, Torah teaches that God pauses, and
notices and appreciates what has come forth. This happens not
only at the end of each day of creation, but also after the very
first act of creation. After bringing forth light, God pauses to
regard what has come forth. As the text teaches, "God saw that
the light was *ki tov*—it was good."¹ This statement of articulated goodness follows right after God's initial act of creativity,
the many "days" of work, and numerous steps, in the process
of forming the world. God does not wait until the entire
cosmos has been formed, or even until an entire ecosystem
has been shaped, before beholding and proclaiming the
goodness of creation. Instead, God takes the first opportunity
possible to praise even this first, formative step.

The word "*ki*" in "*ki tov*" can have different meanings.
Although traditionally, this statement has been read as saying,
"God saw that the light was good," "*ki*" allows for the possibility
to read the Hebrew as referring to the act of seeing itself
("God saw the light") as good. In this reading, what is good in
this first act of creation is not only the light that God brings
forth, but the very fact that God acknowledges it as such.
Similarly, the act of seeing, witnessing, beholding, and appreciating our creative process is essential and nourishing. In
fact, God's creative process is bookended by this act of pausing
and appreciating the good, as it says at the end of the creation
story, "God saw all that God had made and it was very good."²

---

1   Genesis 1:4.
2   Genesis 1:31.

In our own lives, and in our creative process, how often do we allow ourselves the time and space to appreciate what has come through? Can we celebrate the many small steps of creating along the way, rather than waiting until the entire project is complete to appreciate what we've accomplished? One lesson we can learn from God's pronouncement of *"ki tov"* is that "good" is not a status or quality that is determined by others, but rather it is our own ability to discern the manifestation of our own light in the world; like God's light on the first day of creation, it is the first glimmer of what has come through our creative process. And, though this may not be the end of our journey, it is worthy of our acknowledgment and appreciation. To say *"ki tov"* is to acknowledge and give thanks for the flow of energy moving through us into our creations and out into the world. It is to appreciate each stage of the creative process as we are in it. It is to shift the meaning of "good" from "perfect," or "complete," to "what's here for me now in this moment."

To pause and appreciate the creative process is itself a creative act, foundational to the formation of the world. And so, as beings created in the Divine image, may we too remember to regard our own life and creative process with the same generosity, awareness, and appreciation. May you fall in love with both the mess and marvel of yourself and your life. May you open your mind and heart to others and to the world and to what arises in your creative process. And may you find it all *ki tov*.

Acknowledgments

My heart is so full of gratitude for the many people, places, lineages, and traditions that helped *The Place of All Possibility* come into being.

I am so grateful for the Jewish Studio Project team (past and present). Each and every one of you brings such care, humility, humor, and creativity to this work. I am blessed to get to work among such thoughtful and wise humans; I have learned so much from each of you. A particular thanks to Adam Sher for the countless rounds of editing, researching, and thought partnership, for your expansive consciousness and unquenchable passion for this book—I am so grateful. Thank you to the JSP Board for believing in me and in this work; none of this would be possible without you. I am so grateful for the JSP community, each one of you who shows up in person and online, for your energy and presence, and for the ways we collectively weave this work into our lives and into the world. And thank you to the incredible JSP Facilitators and Fellows for entering this lineage and letting the Process grow and evolve through you. It is my deepest hope that, above all, this book serves and supports you in all the creative and courageous ways you bring the Process out into the world.

I am indebted to the richness of Torah and Jewish texts, and to the many people I have been blessed to learn with and from over the years. Thank you to my rabbinical school

teachers at Hebrew College for instilling in me a deep love
of Torah and for helping me learn how to access her depths,
and to my classmates, now colleagues, from that time.
Your Torah lives in me in such profound ways. I am grateful
for all the times you were willing to play and experiment
with me during the conception of the Jewish Studio Process.
You are forever woven into this work.

This book would not have been possible without the
incredible team at Ayin Press. When I first started writing this
book, Ayin didn't yet exist. It truly feels like a blessing from
the universe that this press emerged just as the ideas in this
book grew ready for their next step. Ayin team, the work you
are doing is visionary and I feel so blessed to be among your
writers. Eden Pearlstein, who could have known back in 2006
when your sister brought us together for lunch in Berkeley
that twenty years later we'd be making a book together?
Thank you for taking this project on, for believing in me, and
for the depth and irreverence and everything in between.

Thank you to the many advisors and coaches who read
this work at various stages over the past three years, especially
to my dear friend Noa Silver, whose incisive edits turned
what were pages of writing into a book; to the fierce-hearted
Wild Wednesday Writers group; and to the countless thinkers
and writers whose work inspired and informed this book.

To Joni Blinderman and the folks at The Covenant
Foundation, from the bottom of my heart, thank you for saying
"yes." It is your support that allowed this book to move from a
dream into a reality. And to Dan Libenson and everyone at
Lippman Kanfer Foundation for Living Torah, thank you for
helping to bring this book more fully into the world.

Over the span of three years, this book was written alongside oceans, mountains, forests, and streams—thank you to the
many ecosystems and creatures who accompanied, sustained,
and inspired me through the various stages of writing. To the
plants growing through the sidewalks in my neighborhood,
the moon that kept me company while up writing at 2:00 a.m.,

the ocean lapping at the shore reregulating my nervous system, and the hummingbirds outside my window who—in their search for nectar called me back, again and again, to the life-giving sweetness of text and tradition, even when it felt hard to find.

I don't have words to adequately express my gratitude to my family, without whom this book would not have been possible. Thank you for bearing with me through the long hours, sleepless nights, and many family vacations spent writing and editing. To my kids, Remy and Tovi, thank you for being my biggest cheerleaders and for teaching me, every day, what it means to love. Thank you to my dad for instilling in me the values of both conviction and curiosity, and for supporting me at every juncture of my growth and development. To Jeff for being my co-parent, codirector, best friend, and partner in all things. Thank you for believing in this book when I couldn't and for the love, playfulness, and care you show me and the kids every day. Finally, thank you to my mom. You are my deepest teacher, mentor, collaborator, guide, and confidant. Thank you for the channel that you open to the Divine and for all the ways you've taught me to do the same.

Kosi revayah, my cup overflows. Thank you, thank you, thank you.

To explore more resources related to *The Place of All Possibility*, please visit *www.theplaceofallpossibilitybook.com*.

Rabbi Adina Allen is a spiritual leader, writer, and educator who grew up in an art studio where she learned firsthand the power of creativity for connecting to self and to the Sacred. She is cofounder and creative director of Jewish Studio Project (JSP), an organization that is seeding a future in which every person is connected to their creativity as a force for healing, liberation, and social transformation. Based on the work of her mother, renowned art therapist Pat B. Allen, Adina developed the Jewish Studio Process, a methodology for unlocking creativity, which she has brought to thousands of organizational and community leaders, educators, artists, and clergy across the country. A national media contributor, popular speaker, and workshop leader, Adina has published in scholarly as well as mainstream publications, and more of her writing can be found on her website at *www.adina-allen.com*. She and her family live in Berkeley, California.

Ayin Press is an artist-run publishing platform and production studio rooted in Jewish culture and emanating outward.

Both online and in print, we seek to celebrate artists and thinkers at the margins and explore the growing edges of collective consciousness through a diverse range of mediums and genres.

Ayin was founded on a deep belief in the power of culture and creativity to heal, transform, and uplift the world we share and build together. We are committed to amplifying a polyphony of voices from within and beyond the Jewish world.

For more information about our current or upcoming projects and titles, reach out to us at *info@ayinpress.org*.

To make a tax-deductible contribution to our work, visit our website at *www.ayinpress.org/donate*.